The Fabulous Tom Mix

The
Fabulous
TOM MIX

by OLIVE (STOKES) MIX

with ERIC HEATH

PRENTICE-HALL, INC.
Englewood Cliffs, N.J.

Acknowledgments

Our deep appreciation is extended to Sid Jordan, Joe DeLong, Sam Garrett, and Johnnie Mullens, for their reminiscences of "riding the range" with Tom Mix; also to Sara Hamilton, *Photoplay Magazine*, Norman Katkov, and *Saga Magazine*, for their splendid contributions to this volume.

Contents

The Fabulous Tom Mix

1 ᦰ

Lights! Camera! Action!

THE WOLF WAS AS BIG AS A PONY AND AS SLEEK AS A GREY-hound. There was snow on his head and along his bony backline and on his tail, and he looked like a specter in the Klondike cabin lit only by a single flickering lamp. His hunger had brought him into the cabin, but his cowardice held him motionless for a moment just inside the open door as he watched the astonished prospector. The wind wailed, driving a screen of snow before it into the cabin. The wilderness night was black, and bitter cold.

The man was unarmed. A table was between him and the wolf but that was his only protection. The animal waited for the man to attack. When he did not, when he made no move, the wolf moved forward.

The man retreated, reaching behind him for a weapon, but finding none. He dared not turn around to search and thereby put his back to the wolf who favored, above all else, such a target. The man kept groping behind him as he retreated, until at last his hand felt a chair. He clutched it firmly, his eyes on the wolf. Just as the man gripped the chair, the beast made his move.

The wolf leaped in a ravenous rush, forepaws outstretched to throw the man, fangs bared to rip him. The wolf soared up, all the way up, and over the table, his slavering mouth wide for the kill. But the man had the chair. As the wolf came on, he stepped adroitly to one side like a matador eluding a raging bull. Setting himself in a firm stance, he hit the wolf with the chair, swinging it in a wide arc from right to left, stopping the wolf in mid-air.

The chair shattered, the wood splintering against the beast's skull. The animal fell heavily to the floor of the cabin.

The man finished his swing and, without pausing, launched another, bringing what remained of the chair down upon the still fighting wolf. Finally only a chair leg remained in his hand.

He hit the wolf a third time, carefully keeping his back to the camera as he had been instructed.

"CUT!" shouted the director excitedly.

Wearing the puttees and whipcord breeches that were standard equipment in movie circles in 1910, the director dashed out from behind his protective steel screen. For this was a movie set. The cabin had no roof, the snow was shredded cotton, the wind was a huge fan. Only two small items were real: the wild wolf and the courage of Tom Mix, who had just dropped him.

"Great job! Great!" the director enthused, seizing the chair leg. "They've never seen anything like this. I'll make history with this picture. A *real* wolf!"

"I don't know if he's dead," said Tom Mix, the star of the picture.

"Of course he's dead!" the director shouted. "He's as dead as a doornail! We'll start riots with this one! Killing a live wolf with bare hands!"

"I used a chair," Tom Mix objected.

"Chair! Did you have a gun? No!"

One of the property men, thinking the wolf was dead, moved over to scrutinize the beast. At that instant the wolf recovered consciousness. It had not been killed. It sank its fangs in the leg of the property man, who pulled away and ran off scene screaming with pain.

"Out of the way!" shouted Tom to the director and crew, frozen with terror.

Tom darted forward and pushed the table over on top of the wolf. He tore a leg from one end of the table. As the wolf emerged from beneath the board, Tom hit him between the eyes, again and again, until at last the beast lay still.

It wasn't the last time Tom Mix was to dispose of an evil adversary. When the man who was to grow in popularity until he became the world's greatest cowboy movie star had finished with an enemy, the wretch was dead for always!

There were other harrowing scenes to be shot that day, and it was a long time till the director dismissed his cast and crew. As Tom Mix and I drove home, Tom chatting as cheerily as if he were a different sort of person and had settled a big deal over the telephone from behind an executive's desk in a luxurious office, I wondered once again whether I had been married for nearly a year to a real human being or to some fabu-

lous demigod, and I couldn't help thinking back to the day in
St. Louis when I had first laid eyes on Tom Mix.

Will Rogers grinned and extended one hand to me as he
scratched his head with the other in his fashion so familiar to
me and which was to be known all over the world in later
years.

"Olive Stokes! What in the world are you doing here?"

"I'll have you know that I'm having an exhibition of one of
my pictures at the Fair," I replied.

"You can always bet on a Stokes!" he exclaimed. He had
been very close friends with my parents out in Oklahoma. We
both carried Cherokee blood in our veins as a further bond
between our families.

He turned and beckoned to a dark, slender and very handsome young man who was standing nearby practicing with a
lasso.

"Come here, Tom," he called.

When the young man came up, Will Rogers chuckled.

"Here's how they grow them in Oklahoma, Tom. As pretty
as the country itself. Olive Stokes, this is Tom Mix."

Tom's dark eyes seemed to bore through me as he shook my
hand and muttered, "Howdy, ma'am."

I suppose I may have blushed—for girls did blush in those
days—but if I did, it was more because this unexpected intro-
duction had disturbed my mood, than because I felt any immediate attraction to Will's friend. My father, whom I adored,
had died just a few weeks before, and the shock of losing him
had plunged me into an abyss of grief from which I was just
emerging. It had changed me from a carefree and sometimes
intransigent ranch child, as wild as the country of my birth, into a sober girl reaching for maturity.

As the three of us sauntered over to a bench in front of a
sign reading ZACK MULHALL'S WILD WEST SHOW, I

found myself ignoring Tom and practically forgetting he was even there—although I did notice how he kept playing with the rope he was holding. Later I learned that he couldn't sit still without doing something with his hands.

My trip to St. Louis—I had come there to receive an award for a painting of mine that was being exhibited in the Indian Territory building at the Fair—was my first real venture into the world since that awful period of sorrow.

Will was soon making me laugh again. "I'm going to take you to dinner," he announced, "and tomorrow show you the Fair."

"That wouldn't be right," broke in Tom.

As he spoke the rather embarrassing realization dawned on me that he hadn't been given a chance to say much within the last half-hour. I discovered later that he wasn't a heavy talker on any occasion. "I'd be pleased if you'd do *me* the honor of showing you around the Fair," Tom added.

"Reckon we can trust him, Olive?" Will winked.

It was show time by then, and the two men left me to get ready for their entrances. I took my place in the audience of the Mulhall Wild West Show. Both Will and Tom gave thrilling performances, though they were only in their middle twenties then, and the great years of stardom for them were yet to come. To me they were as great as Buffalo Bill had ever been.

Already I was sorry my visit to St. Louis was only for one day. The following afternoon I would have to return to school in Nashville, Tennessee. I did not have much time to become properly acquainted with either Tom or Will.

Will took me to dinner that evening, and we had a gay time talking about our beloved northeastern section of Oklahoma. He recalled how my father would sit with a pair of binoculars in his little office in our ranch house and keep watch on everything that was going on, and how he kept large sums of money in a tin box in his desk drawer without the slightest fear of anyone stealing it.

Promptly at nine Will returned me to the Jefferson Hotel, where Lyman T. Hay, the manager, was waiting to see me safely in for the night. My unchaperoned trip to St. Louis had been made possible only because Lyman, an old friend of my father's, had promised to keep an eye on me.

As Will and I stood in the lobby chatting for a moment before he left, I ventured: "Do you think Mr. Mix was just joking about showing me around the Fair tomorrow?"

"Don't think you have a bit of cause to worry about that," Will replied, his bright eyes twinkling.

I discovered that this was true enough. When I came downstairs for breakfast the next morning, Tom was in the lobby waiting for me. It wasn't until a good many years later that Will told me Tom had waited there for me all night. But by then I too knew of his determination to accomplish any purpose that he set out to achieve!

I must honestly admit that I was more interested in the Fair itself that day than in my slender "tall, dark and handsome" escort. Forest Park was alive with excitement and swarming crowds.

There was a refreshing international air about the buildings of French-classic design and the foreign and domestic exhibits.

In my exuberance to try to see everything—an impossible feat to accomplish in one short day—Tom was led a chase around the park that would have left a less physically endowed man puffing and irritated.

Although I *thought* myself a full woman, probably Tom looked upon me as a country child taking a city sabbatical.

Later in the day, when we finally paused for breath at the Cherokee exhibit, I realized that I'd been babbling all day about myself and had learned almost nothing about my escort.

I laughed. "We haven't much time left for you to tell me about yourself."

His face lit up with a wonderful, meaningful smile that seemed to come up from deep inside him. In the future I was to learn that everything Tom did came from deep inside him. He was a man of feelings and actions, not fancy words.

"I think you're going to learn all about me some day," he said.

That was all.

The man of mystery, I decided. Rather an exciting thought!

Before I knew it, the time arrived for me to leave for the station. We rushed to the show tent for a breathless farewell with Will. He apologized for not being able to go with me to the train, but some business had come up to prevent him. I didn't know then that Tom had contrived this "business" excuse with Will.

We barely made the train on time.

"Thank you so much," I said to Tom, raising my voice above the commotion on the station platform. "And it's been so nice meeting you." I felt warm with excitement. "In case I don't see you again—well, I want to wish you luck."

He smiled. "You'll be seeing me again."

Then we shook hands, longer than was necessary. The train shrieked its final warning and I couldn't delay another moment.

Tom followed my car down the platform as the train moved out. I kept waving and he kept smiling. I kept my nose pressed against the window glass until he disappeared from view. Slowly the remainder of the people on the platform moved past the window. Streets with trees, houses and roads flowed past, fastest near the car, slower farther away. I sank back against the red plush upholstery of the seat and closed my eyes. Probably, I thought, I will never see him again!

For the next four years (1904–1908) I was busy completing the long process of becoming a woman. Then when I had completed my formal education I returned to our ranch to assume part of the managerial responsibilities. My mother, who since the death of my father had grown more and more bewildered by business details, needed my help.

Our ranch, where I was born in 1890, was in the northeastern section of Oklahoma, an extension of the Ozark Plateau, a beautiful region of richly timbered hills, green valleys, clear streams. It was a man's country and I had sensed the masculinity of it in my childhood, when I had been a fearful tomboy. My mother, of Cherokee Indian and Scotch-Irish antecedents, had once asked me: "Olive, don't you want to grow up to be a fine lady? You can't," she added, "act like a boy and expect to end up a great lady."

But it was a country to be a man in, and I wasn't particularly interested in Mother's hopes for me. I was going to be a male in spite of petticoats.

When I was six years old my temerity led me to climb on a bronco from the corral fence. The ride was brief and lively, and the broken collarbone I ended with was very painful.

"She'll grow out of this wildness," my father said in consoling my mother.

My brother Dick Stokes and my Uncle Pete had the greatest influence on my development during those early years. They managed to lead me into most of the trouble I got into. Dick was four years older than I, and Pete was seven years older. Pete was my father's youngest brother and had lived with us since I was very tiny. The two were in collusion, it seemed, to make life a series of agonies for me.

"Now don't you follow us today," they would say to me as they ran off on their long legs.

And I would promptly follow them.

I was six when they presented me with a black furry carcass at the sawmill.

"Poor dead kitty," said Dick with a very solemn face. "Why don't you take it home and bury it, Olive?"

I did. I went marching into the kitchen with that dead skunk. My mother instantly lost her serenity. It was the only time I ever heard her shriek. The skunk was disposed of promptly and I found myself in the bathtub before I could turn around. Under Mother's unflagging eye I spent a great part of the following week becoming sterilized.

The boys hollered with glee over that.

But I didn't learn. Among other things, the boys sent me home one day with dead rats tied to my belt. I thought it was very funny at the time, but Mother didn't. And she saw no humor either in my deathly experience with chewing tobacco. The boys had told me it was a kind of candy and shoved a great handful into my mouth.

However, my mother didn't completely lose patience until the boys tied me to an unappreciative calf one day and I ended up with another broken collarbone.

"She'll grow as wild as the Cherokee Strip if we don't steady her," my mother told Father.

"I guess it is high time she's sent off to school," he admitted with a touch of melancholy in his voice. "That'll plant some tameness in her."

Life on the ranch left a deep imprint that could never be displaced by any number of frilly early-century dresses or finishing schools. I wouldn't have wanted it that way. There was a rich scope to life in those days that has never been exactly paralleled since.

It was a life full of breathtaking beauty, of majestic landscape and fresh loveliness, especially in the spring when the ranch burst with redbud, dogwood and wild blue indigo. It was a life of energy and ceaseless dawn-to-dusk work, with quiet evenings of singing around the great stone fireplace in

our parlor. For some—for the new settlers—it was a life of lean
times until the discovery of oil in 1903 changed the entire com-
plexion of the region.

I found I was growing up. My brother and uncle treated
me with new respect when they found I could outride both of
them, either bareback or in saddle. After proving my ability
to kill rattlers with the same bold finesse they used, I was
suddenly no longer "little sister" and "little niece." I had arrived. By the time I was ten, the ranch hands, by conspiracy or
otherwise, were calling me "Princess" and treating me like one.
My woman's heart must have been developing in me, for I was
very pleased with it all.

Now I look back upon these younger years of mine, I like
to think I see a plan superior to mine present in them and
directing them. For without them I should never have been
able to meet on common ground, and share the life of, the
man who as my husband was to complete my life.

For when I returned to the ranch I, like all other girls, had
dreams of love and marriage. At times in the past I had thought
about Tom Mix and lived in hope that some day a letter
would come from him. But none came.

Evidently he had completely forgotten me and yet I could
never forget what he had said: "You'll be seeing me again."
They were his last words when the train pulled out of St. Louis.
Strangely, this man of silence and mystery kept lurking as
an intriguing vision in my mind.

In December, 1908, I took the long trip to Medora, North
Dakota, to buy some horses for the ranch. Old friends of our
family who lived there had written about some excellent
horses that could be purchased very reasonably.

Nels and Katrine Nichols had not seen me since their visit
to our ranch years before. When they met me at the station
in Medora, Nels greeted me with a smile. "For land's sake,
how you've changed!"

I was shivering as they helped me into their buggy, despite my heavy fur coat. I had been forewarned of the sub-zero temperatures of western North Dakota, but wasn't wholly prepared for the icy blast that swept in from the ranges and penetrated to my bones.

"You'll get used to it," laughed Katrine as we drove off.

Nels and Katrine got me settled in their big rambling house on the outskirts of the town. I quickly plunged into a round of familiar activities. This was frontier country too, and though the terrain was different from Oklahoma, the way of living was much the same as that I had been used to.

Nels Nichols reminded me of my father—not that he looked like him, but he had the same kind heart and trust in humanity. Katrine was a bubbling, effervescent little woman, a dynamo of energy. She was always planning parties or dances and was very concerned that I did not seem to have any particular interest in men.

It was on a sparkling bright day about a week before Christmas that Nels, Katrine and I went to the railway station to meet Luke Bells, an assistant overseer at our ranch, who had come to Medora to help me in the final selection and shipment of the horses I was going to purchase.

Luke was on the train all right, just as expected.

And a tall, slender, smiling man got off right behind him.

"Tom Mix!" I sputtered.

I knew I must be blushing furiously, for everyone laughed at my utter confusion.

Tom, grinning now, moved right up to me and swept off his hat. "I told you we'd be meeting again some day. And here we are—and you're all grown up."

At that moment I wasn't quite sure of my feelings. Perhaps I was a little angry with him for bowing into my life so briefly four years ago, and then stepping out of it until now, with no word in between.

I could not deny that I was glad to see him.

"Tom's here because he wouldn't give me any peace until I let him come along," explained Luke. "He was at the ranch looking for you."

Nels told Luke and Tom that the best place to stay would be the Cowboy Hotel and apologized for not having room for them at the ranch.

"Some of the ranch hands even have to sleep on the floor in the kitchen," he explained.

Before anything else, Tom and Luke had to come to the Nichols home for dinner. Katrine, with the help of Mattie, her housekeeper, prepared a special dinner of Norwegian dishes: *lutefish*, a cod dish which was her specialty; *lefse*, unleavened potato bread; and *fattigmand*, a delicious Norwegian pastry fried in deep fat.

Tom had about three helpings of everything, although he had eyed the food suspiciously when it was first served to him.

He winked at Katrine. "How about Olive?" he asked. "Can she cook? A woman ought to be able to cook."

"Of course I can cook, Tom Mix!" I said a little testily, and then remembered that Tom had a great deal to learn about me—and I certainly had even more to learn about him.

We started our "education" right the next morning when we rode out to the ranch of a big horse-raiser, Sam Short, to look at his stock. It was a harrowing ride through the craggy, hole-ridden badlands, that enormous stretch of buttes and eroded land that fans out from Medora. The badlands are beautiful with their shifting colors and sweeping, lonely vistas; but they are terrifying too, when you are caught on them in the midst of a swirling, blinding blizzard as we were that day.

I was proud of the way I handled my horse and myself through that exciting journey, and made no protests even though my heart was hammering.

When the storm finally abated, Tom said, "You're quite a woman, Olive."

If my face hadn't been almost frozen, I probably would have colored.

"Go on with your folderol," I said, trying to make light of it. But there, out in the midst of those desolate, freezing badlands, I was suddenly feeling warm.

We were given a most gracious welcome at the Short ranch and immediately drawn into the family. Nels and Katrine were due for a visit in a few days to enter into the Christmas festivities. Luke came out early and he, Tom and I spent the mornings riding out on the snow-swept plains to look over the horses. Soon it got to be just Tom and I, and I was sure it was Tom who had suggested to Luke that he make himself scarce. For Luke was always missing when we were ready for our ride.

But I didn't care. I guess it was the way I wanted it too.

I kept wondering if there would be an awakening some morning to find that Tom had vanished from my life again. He seemed to be a restless man, and our relationship certainly wasn't a clearly defined thing to me at that point.

I skidded around the subject. "How long are you planning to stay in these parts, Tom?"

He gave me one of those slow, meaningful smiles of his. "Till my plans are settled," he replied. "That might be any time now."

What did he mean by "plans"? Was I to be included in them? Or did he look forward exclusively to his work? Before he had come to Medora he had finished a long run with the Miller Brothers' 101 Ranch Wild West Show. During our rides he would tell me about that tremendous ranch with its half-million acres of land.

He told me that while he was in training for the 101 Ranch Show, he was strolling down the street of the nearby town one night, and as he walked along kept practicing the art of making

a quick draw with his gun and "throwing it down" on imaginary targets. When he came to an alley, to his surprise, two
rough-looking men came out with their hands up! As it turned
out they were a couple of robbers at work on the back door
of a hardware store! Through sheer coincidence he had drawn
his gun, pointed it directly at them, and thus held them for
the law.

Aside from glimpses of his past at that time I only got one
other episode out of him—about his career as one of the Rough
Riders in the Philippines. He told me that he was with a de-
tachment sent out on a scouting trip into the jungles. There
they were set upon by the enemy and several of them were
killed. It took Tom days to make his way back to camp. When
he arrived he found his buddies, who had assumed him either
killed or captured, dividing up his personal possessions among
themselves.

"I got about half sore when they did that!" grinned Tom.

During Christmas week Tom scarcely left my side while we
participated in the exhausting but exhilarating celebration
that lasted from Christmas to New Year's Day, and encom-
passed almost the entire ranching community before we were
finished.

The celebration began with a big square dance. I was itching to show off my dancing accomplishments to Tom and was
in a state of feverish anticipation while the guests kept arriving on horseback all day in groups of two to ten. They traveled
through an endless snow falling from leaden skies. In the winter people did not travel alone in the badlands. But they did
travel, under any conditions, when there was fun to be had or
work to be done.

It's hard to believe that the dance lasted almost twenty-
four hours. We danced in relays. After a two- or three-hour
sprint on the floor we would lie down and rest while another

group wore themselves out on the mountain waltzes and polkas and the stamping of square dances that rocked the ranch house.

I whirled and pranced joyously in Tom's arms while the caller sang out such typical calls of those days as:

> Break trail home
> In Indian style
> Swing the gal behind you
> Once in a while
> Now grab your partner
> And go hog wild.

I felt closer to Tom that night than ever before. It was flattering that he monopolized me for every dance and insisted I refuse other offers.

I thought it was going to be the perfect night.

"Olive," Tom said during an intermission, "what do you expect to do with your life?"

Here it comes, I thought somewhat fearfully.

"That depends," I said evasively. I had visions of Tom kneeling on the floor and asking for my hand.

"I suppose you'll be getting married one of these days," he said. "That's about all women think about, isn't it?"

I flushed. I didn't know whether he was laughing under that stony expression or not. "Maybe *some* women do," I said.

"But not you, huh?" he said tauntingly. "Well, I guess there are advantages to staying single too—even for a woman. Single life sure doesn't hurt a *man* much."

I was furious as I looked at his unrevealing face. But his dark eyes were twinkling provocatively as he swept me off to another dance.

The game of evasion went on until New Year's Day, when the week-long celebration at the Short ranch came to a roistering end. By that time, I had completed my selection of the horses I was going to buy from the Shorts. Bill McCarty, who had been a guest at the Shorts' all week and who was an old friend of Tom's, invited me then to spend a week at his ranch to look over his stock.

"I don't expect you'll be needing me over there," laughed Luke, as he left to return to Medora with Nels and Katrine.

Everyone, it seemed, already thought it a foregone conclusion that Tom and I were a "pair" and that the ultimate outcome was inevitable. Everyone except me. I was in a state of complete confusion.

If Tom ever was going to say anything, the "short" twenty-mile ride along the Little Missouri River to Bill's ranch should have provided the opportunity. Midway, I reined up to rest.

"This is certainly a lonely looking country," I remarked while gazing around at the vast endlessness of the snow-shrouded buttes. In that bleak dead whiteness it seemed hardly possible that this treeless land was a myriad reflection of red, blue and yellow mustard in the summer and that the nutritive matting of buffalo grass that supported the vast stock-raising ranches would once again appear in the plains.

"No country's really lonely when you're around your own kind of people," Tom remarked.

I nodded in agreement and waited for him to designate me as "his kind of people." But nothing came. The heat of anger rose in me, despite the cold weather, and I heard Tom chuckle under his breath as we rode on.

Our week at Bill McCarty's place was a week of languid, gentle quiet, with one exception. One morning Tom, Bill, and I were out moving around the corrals when I spotted a beautiful black horse alone in a small enclosure, moving with great grace and nervous energy. When it reared its handsome head, I said to Bill, "There's a horse I'd like to have."

He grinned. "Not that one. He's a killer! Nobody's ever been able to break him yet and one of the boys went to the hospital with a broken back trying to do it. I'm thinking of turning him loose when the weather warms up."

Tom moved over to the enclosure and eyed the horse.

"Have your men saddle him up and get him out of the corral," he said. "I can break him for you."

Bill shook his head. "I don't want you to get hurt, Tom. He's a demon . . . has a habit of rearin' up and falling back on his rider."

The upshot was that the horse was finally saddled and with the help of two men taken outside of the enclosure for Tom to show his stuff.

"Never try breaking a horse like this in a corral," advised Tom. "Maybe that's one reason your boys couldn't do it."

Several of the ranch hands and Mrs. McCarty had gathered around to watch.

Tom moved over and with lightning speed jumped into the saddle. At the same instant he gave a piercing yell and banged the horse's head with his sombrero.

The horse was so startled at Tom's method that instead of rearing up and doing its tricks, it started off across the plains as though trying to escape from the devil.

Tom and the horse disappeared behind a clump of trees. About a half-hour later he came back on a very different "black demon." The stallion was flecked with white froth from what had very evidently been a long and strenuous gallop. Apparently it was as gentle as a kitten.

"Well, I'll be danged!" I heard Bill McCarty mutter.

Tom rode the horse into the corral, and after giving it a soothing pat on the neck and a few words of friendship, came over to me with a grin. "You can buy him now, Olive."

In the afternoons Tom and Bill generally had target practice
on the brown prairie chickens that rested in clusters on the
stockade. Tom was a crack shot.

The evenings were full of song, a frontier tradition I was
used to and loved. We sat before the great roaring fire while
Bill played the banjo and his hired man Mack strummed a
guitar. We must have covered every old favorite that week.
Tom was partial to Stephen Foster and he sang the famous
ballads in a rich baritone voice full of emotional nuances.

The McCartys had a pet hog, a big Poland China they called
Charlie. It would come to the kitchen door, grunt and push at
it. Someone would let it in and it would go over and lie down
in front of the fireplace.

One evening Tom looked over at the sleeping hog and said,
"Let's sing one for Charlie. It'll save getting up and putting
him out." But the singing did not cause Charlie to budge. In
fact, he seemed to like it.

At last the final selection of horses had been made and there
was simply no excuse for me to stay on at the ranch house.
Tom and I returned to Medora, where we were swept up in
another round of activities. Nels and Katrine seemed to be in
conspiracy to keep us so busy that Tom and I scarcely had a
moment to be alone together.

I was due to go home on January 20, 1909, and the calen-
dar turned with a swift, cruel rush toward that date. Each
day my hopes fell another notch.

The crowning blow fell on January 19, the day before I
was to leave. Nels and Katrine had arranged a big farewell
dance for me that night at the Cowboy Hotel and I assumed,
of course, that Tom would be my escort.

I was amazed and furious when Tom announced to me that
he was taking a Medora woman—a young widow—to the dance.

"I kind of have an obligation to her," he explained with a

perfectly straight face. "She was the wife of an old friend of mine. Hope you don't mind."

My face blazed, then blanched. "Mind?" I forced a weak smile. "Why should I mind, Tom?"

I heeled quickly and flew to my room, thinking bitterly that when I left on the following day I would have to start putting Tom Mix out of my mind and heart for good. I was too angry even to be suspicious when Luke asked me to go to the dance with him. Despite my quavering emotions, I determined to have a good time. If it was the last thing I ever did, I would show Tom Mix that I simply didn't care!

I took supreme pleasure in informing Tom, when he asked me to dance, that my program was filled, *entirely* filled!

Right after that he disappeared and so did Nels Nichols. I had not as yet seen the "widow" Tom had taken to the dance. Had he gone out with her somewhere?

I flitted around the ballroom floor, laughing brightly and telling myself that I was having the best time of my life. When I speak of "ballroom" it was really the dining room of the Cowboy Hotel, but the chairs and tables had been pushed back against the wall and the floor had been waxed, and there were plenty of lanterns and bunting to bring gaiety and color to the place.

While Luke was waltzing with me, he saw me looking around the room.

"What's the matter, Olive?" he asked. "Looking for someone?"

I sensed he was trying to be cute. "No. Just wondering what happened to Nels and Katrine."

The moment came for the playing of "Good Night, Ladies," and Luke and I got our coats and left the hotel.

It was bitter cold outside, but there was a full moon and the stars glittered like diamonds. The Nicholses' house was only a short distance from the Cowboy Hotel. The dance had left me tired and moody and I paid little attention to Luke's occasional remarks.

We reached the house and Luke bade me good night. As I started up the steps I heard the sound of talking and laughing, and turned to see Tom, Nels and Katrine come up the path.

Nels bustled up to me. "Come on, Olive," he boomed. "We've got business to take care of in the kitchen."

He led me through the immense living room and into the spacious kitchen. As usual some of the ranch hands were sleeping on the floor along the walls, snuggled up in their round-up beds and apparently utterly oblivious to anything.

When I entered the kitchen, followed by Tom and Katrine, Mattie, the housekeeper, was placing a big cake on the kitchen table which was already laden with cold cuts of meat and different edibles. Something over my head attracted my attention and I looked up to see some Chinese lanterns dangling from strings tied to the beamed ceiling.

"What's this?" I demanded. "Who's celebrating what?"

Katrine looked as if she were about to cry, and Tom looked very stern.

Nels Nichols walked over in front of a big sideboard which stood against the wall.

"All right, Tom," he said. "You and Olive stand over here in front of me. Katrine, you stand next to Olive."

Tom reached out his hand to me. I went over and stood next to him facing Nels Nichols.

Another fun game, I decided. I started to giggle.

"Don't laugh, Olive," Tom said. "This is serious business!"

Somewhere in another room someone was playing the Mendelssohn "Wedding March" on the piano.

Nels started reading from a little black book. I didn't pay much attention to what he was saying until he asked solemnly: "Do you, Olive Stokes, take this man to be thy wedded husband, to live together under God's ordinance . . . ?"

As Nels Nichols pronounced the words I stared at him and then looked at Tom. He was gazing very sternly at Nels. I glanced around at Katrine. She was wiping her eyes.

"All right," I decided to myself, "I'll go along with the fun." So I replied in a loud, firm voice, "I do!" and smiled to show I could be a good sport.

"*. . . I now pronounce you . . . man and wife. . . .*"

"What's next?" I asked with a little laugh. At that instant Tom reached over and put his arm around me and kissed me.

I pulled back, my face crimson. "Say . . . !" I sputtered, not knowing whether to be mad or what.

"Come on, everybody!" exclaimed Tom, as he shoved me toward the table. "Let's eat, drink and be married!"

Later that night when I discovered something I had never known before—that Nels Nichols was a Justice of the Peace and that his brother was County Clerk—and that the reason Tom, Nels and Katrine had left the dance was to carry out a put-up job of getting the marriage license and prepare for the wedding—I was too dazed to think straight.

The whole world was a peculiarly weird and yet somehow lovely maze. A voice kept saying: "You're married to Tom. . . . You're married to Tom. . . ."

But I did manage to say to him, "The least thing you could have done was to say you loved me!"

2

Roaming Days

THERE WAS THE USUAL AURA OF EXTERNAL EXCITEMENT that goes with a wedding celebration, accompanied in my case with a trembling inner turmoil. Here I was, plunged into a marriage with a man whom I really knew only superficially. It takes time to probe deeply, and Tom and I had barely cut the surface on each other.

All those tender moments of courtship, which all girls thrill about, had been lacking. But Tom took a different point of view. "I've always believed," he said, "in having more of that kind of thing after marriage instead of before. It's getting so that most folks lose all the enchantment by the time they are hitched."

Maybe he had something!

I switched the subject and demanded to know why he thought I would go along with everything.

"I generally get what I want and keep it," he replied.

In future years I was to discover that he really did get what he wanted—but many times he found out that he wasn't sure he wanted to keep it.

In the pre-dawn hour after our wedding I was breathless with excitement over our planless future together, as we waited at the railroad station for the train that was to take us to Miles City, Montana, for the first leg of our honeymoon.

I looked over at Tom and laughed. "I still can't believe it's real!"

Tom pinched my arm. "That's so you'll know it's real," he laughed. "And it didn't happen so fast. I started laying my plans at the St. Louis Fair. I let you slip away from me then to give you time to grow up."

It seemed symbolic to me that we left Medora just as the fresh day was beginning to break. I can remember no other sunrise exactly like that one. It was as though someone were slowly pouring a bottle of wine over the sky. The warm glimmer floated down through the frosty haze and licked at the black, bare buttes with soft fire; and the steep yellow clay cliffs on the edge of town, blackish hulks by night, became a soft melody of shifting colors in the reddening dawn. It was as though this day were born for us alone. *What a wonderful omen for happiness*, I thought as the train pulled out and Tom slipped his hand over mine.

Then, after the first magic of dawn had passed and a matchless blue sky had covered the frosty darkness, I got my tongue back. I turned to Tom and laughed. "Tom, just *why* Miles City?" I had heard of the place, but I doubted that it was the most ideal spot for a honeymoon.

"I've got friends there I want to show you off to," Tom said.

"Do you know everybody everywhere?" I asked jokingly, not knowing how close to the truth I'd come.

Tom winked. "A man makes a lot of friends in his roaming years."

I didn't know then the fantastic scope of Tom's roaming. The entire West was, and had been, his living room. But he hadn't stopped there. His adventures had taken him to Cuba, Africa, the Philippines, and China. I had only had a glimpse of his past life and it was going to be a long time before I learned all about his fantastic background. He was only twenty-nine when we were married, but he had already lived the lives of a dozen men.

I sensed then that I had married a man of heroic stature, but it was to take me years to know the full man. As for Tom's exploits, I usually had to learn of them from his friends, for he never in any circumstances made himself out to be the real Western hero he was. He was entirely devoid of the swagger and braggadocio that have characterized so many lesser heroes before and since.

He really disliked talking about himself. To speak of his accomplishments was downright embarrassing to him. Even after he became famous he tended to minimize his exploits in the accounts he gave the publicity-hungry movie men. He played down his personal accomplishments, but he never deviated a moment from the truth. The deepest seeds in Tom were truth and integrity. These were the qualities that gave him the sweeping bigness of a titan in everything he did.

But on the train that morning I was too busy with my sense of personal happiness to worry much about what made Tom click. I was aware only that it was the most beautiful day since the beginning of the world and now, having been plunged into marriage, I knew that I was in love and was sure Tom had put his "roaming days" behind him. At the moment I visualized Tom and I working together to build up my ranch in Oklahoma, and making it one of the garden spots in the country. I was proud to be able to give our marriage financial security and a bright future. Little did I know then that those "roaming days" were not over for Tom and were just beginning for me!

I sank back against the hard seat and dreamed, while Tom squeezed my hand. However, I was still young enough to be a tiny bit homesick, even on my honeymoon.

I snapped out of my reverie when I felt the pressure of Tom's hand tighten on mine. I looked over at him and followed his eyes to the front of the car where an interesting scene was beginning.

I had noticed a woman and her son, a boy of about ten, when Tom and I boarded the train at Medora. She was a fine-looking woman wearing widow's weeds. Her clothes and the boy's testified they were from some Eastern city.

I had also noticed the man, who until now had been sitting in the middle of the sparsely occupied car, an enormous man in both bulk and height, with a blood-filled face reddened by liquor.

The man had moved over and was standing next to the woman's seat, leaning down to speak to the woman as she huddled toward the window. Her back was rigid with fright.

The boy, sensing danger in this great hulk of a man and heroically deciding to protect his mother, jumped up to push the intruder away—like an ant attacking an elephant.

The man pushed the boy aside. "Get out of my way, runt!" he bellowed. Then he took hold of the woman's arm. "I don't like women who turn their back on me," he exclaimed.

He hardly finished the sentence, for there was suddenly a mountain lion grasping his arm, pulling him deep into the aisle. I liken Tom to a mountain lion because that animal defeats an opponent often many times larger than itself, through wiry precision of movement and tensile strength. So it was with Tom. He was a big man himself—nearly six feet tall and weighing 175—but many of the men of bad character in the West whom he met in tests of decision over the years were literally Vikings.

And so it was with this burly giant that Tom spun like a top in the aisle.

"We don't treat women like that out here," Tom said in his even, controlled voice scarcely modulated by the heat of emergency.

My heart was playing drums, but I managed to pull the train cord. The train whistle shrieked its eerie acknowledgment of the signal as the man began to recover his equilibrium.

"We'll talk this over at the rear of the car," Tom told him.

But the man wasn't having any talking. He snorted with fury and lifted his massive arm with a slashing movement. Tom acted so swiftly I barely saw his fist come down on the man's wrist.

With a yelp of pain the man jerked out a gun with his un-injured hand. Tom gave a lightning-like kick at the weapon and it flew off down the aisle. "We won't settle this with guns," Tom said calmly.

Never in his long career in the West as sheriff, marshal, and cowboy did Tom settle a personal dispute with a gun when it could be settled with hard fists. Though he was quick to act against a wrong—his temper could explode with an in-stancy of a firecracker when his sense of moral justice was violated—every action of his existence was a reasoned action. His brain forever commanded his temper. It was this quality that made him a leader of men, a giant in his own way in the final building of the West.

The fight did not last long. The big bully flayed wildly with his arms, but his knotted, hamlike fists seldom found their target. Tom ducked and bounced like a jaguar, throwing his own fists at the huge man's body with the regularity of a machine gun. The "mountain lion" soon wore down the "elephant." By the time the train ground to a complete stop and the conductor came running in, the burly man was panting groggily on the aisle floor, beside a deck of cards and a pair of dice that had spilled from his pocket.

"We've got a deposit to make," Tom told the startled conductor. He dragged the man by the coat collar and shoved him toward the door. Then he took him out on the platform and dumped him off the train while I picked up the dice and cards and tossed them after him. They scattered like fluff in the prairie wind.

We watched the man reeling dizzily toward a nearby ranch house as the train pulled out.

It was now time for amenities. The woman, still shaking, came back to meet us. Her son was pop-eyed with admiration for Tom. I was to see that expression of consummate adoration for Tom on the faces of thousands and thousands of youngsters in later years.

"I don't even know how to start to thank you," the woman said. She was almost weeping. "I was terrified—"

"Don't you worry any more, Ma'am," said Tom with his reverent respect for women, a respect he shared with countless other men of the West.

Contrary to common conception, the rough-and-ready men of the Old West *did* extend every courtesy to womanhood, except, of course, the rare type of man such as the one Tom had just dusted off the train. There was plenty of rough talk in the Western saloons and bunkhouses, but you never heard an expletive when there was a woman present. If you did, the offender was soon being ground into the dirt by the other men.

The widow was from Philadelphia and she and her son were on their way to Helena, where they were going to live with her brother. Her tenseness told us silently that she might already be considering turning around at the next stop and heading back to Philadelphia.

Tom was quick to modify the fright she had just had. "You're going to be living in the greatest part of the country," he told her. "Won't be long before you'll *feel* that. As for what just happened, it'll never happen again. You'll see."

Tom was right. The chances that the woman would ever again be subjected to violence were slim. Most of the really rough days of the West were history by then and the good people had driven out a lot of the bad ones simply by weight of number and persistence. But even in the earliest pioneer days the good people could live in peace if they had the sense to keep out of the way of the bad ones.

"No matter where you live, there are good ones and bad ones," Tom said. "Out here we get rid of the bad ones fast. Either we get them, or they trip themselves."

In that observation Tom summed up the credo that formed the unchanging moral underlying his later films: the good man reaped his reward and the villain paid for his evil. It was that way in real life, too.

Tom illustrated his point with a story:

"I once was acquainted with a sheriff down at Two Buttes, Colorado," he began. "It was a good clean community, but there'd been trouble with rustlers—outlaws who made it a business of stealing cattle. Finally the sheriff traced the root of the trouble to a man named Russell who had a ranch about fifteen miles out of town. Russell and two Mexicans in his employ had been rustling steers from the other ranchers and taking them across the border."

I looked at the boy, who was sitting forward eagerly in the seat opposite ours, his eyes widening by the second.

"Well, the sheriff rode out to Russell's place alone one day. He didn't have any definite proof on Russell and he wasn't sure how he was going to handle the situation. But the sheriff reckoned a little on human nature. He figured that when you get a rat cornered on his home ground, he'll reveal himself one way or another."

The boy was almost falling off his seat with suspense by now, as Tom continued his story at his usual calm pace.

"Anyway," said Tom, "when Russell and the Mexicans saw the sheriff they must have figured he *did* have proof against them. A man doesn't run and hide when he's guiltless. Well, these men drew their guns and scattered fast when the sheriff rode in. Russell disappeared behind a bunch of loaded hayracks, and the Mexicans ran to barricade themselves in the toolshed."

"How'd the sheriff get them?" squealed the boy eagerly.

"The sheriff didn't want any killing if he could avoid it," Tom continued, smiling at the boy. "He wasn't any different from any other law man in that respect. So first he tried to reason with the men, telling them they'd get a fair trial and a chance if they'd give themselves up peaceably."

"But they *didn't*, did they?" said the boy. It was obvious that the story couldn't end that way.

"No, they didn't," said Tom. "So the sheriff gave them fair warning. He shouted to them that he was coming after them. He headed toward the toolshed, knowing that Russell would take a shot at him from the hayracks. He knew Russell was somewhere behind the long line of racks, but didn't know the exact spot. The only thing the sheriff could hope was that Russell wasn't a good shot. Anyway, the sheriff didn't walk two yards before the shot came."

"Was he killed?" the boy gasped, his eyes popping by now.

"The shot got him in the leg," said Tom. "It also brought Russell out of hiding, which was what the sheriff wanted. Two quick shots from the sheriff and Russell was lying moaning on the ground, a leg and his gun arm out of action."

By now I was as excited as the boy. "What happened to the Mexicans?" I asked.

"Well," said Tom, "the sheriff gave the Mexicans another chance to come out with their hands up. But there was nothing but silence from the toolshed—so he had to kick down the door to go in after them. I guess the Mexicans were surprised at his exposing himself like that. They were just surprised enough—as the sheriff hoped they'd be—to put them off balance for a moment. Their shots got the sheriff, but their fluster made their aim bad, and the sheriff was still standing on his feet when he put the Mexicans out of commission."

"How bad was the sheriff shot up?" asked the boy.

"Oh, he was nicked up a little," chuckled Tom, "but I hear he's still alive."

Nicked up a little! I heard the whole story from Tom's close friend, Sid Jordan, a couple of years later. It was Tom himself, of course, who was really the sheriff of Two Buttes who cleaned up on the rustlers. It was his natural humility and modesty that caused him, in relating the story to the widow and her son, to refer to the hero sheriff as an "acquaintance."

As for being "nicked up a little," Tom's receipts from that affray were a bullet in his thigh, one in his forearm, one in his neck, and one in his head. They were hardly nicks. But Tom probably did look upon those wounds with a truly casual eye. He was wounded countless times and suffered innumerable broken bones before he ever faced his first motion picture camera.

During his early career and while working in pictures, he suffered a fractured shoulder and a broken jaw. Every rib in his body had been broken one or more times, both knee caps fractured, his feet crushed. To the day of his death he carried in his body unremoved buckshot. To add to this collection were several knife wounds. Many doctors marveled how he had lived and carried on such an active life.

Tom's story had done more than point up a moral of obvious truth. The widow was calm and at ease now. There wasn't much danger of her starting back to Philadelphia at the next stop.

As for the boy, a barrel of boiling water couldn't have unglued him from Tom. He clung on, asking Tom seemingly a million questions about range life. I smoldered a little, remembering that this was my wedding journey and that Tom should be talking to *me*.

But I soon stopped smoldering when I reasoned that nothing—even the early hours of a honeymoon—could stop Tom from helping a person in a moment of need. After their frightening experience the widow and her boy needed reassurance, and Tom gave it to them in his own wise way.

I was to see the same sort of thing repeated many times later. Tom always took time for other people. And he never forgot a friend. Years later, when he was at the peak of his movie career, he was still remembering the old range-riding pals of former years. A Tom Mix film never appeared that didn't have some of Tom's old cronies in it.

Tom gave the boy one final big thrill when the train stopped for emergency repairs on the plains about an hour outside Miles City. The boy had been begging Tom to "shoot something." Tom pulled his gun from a valise and found a small can. The four of us got off the train.

The wintry plain stretched before us, flat, gaunt and quivering under the temperamental wind—not ideal conditions for the demonstration of shooting prowess.

Tom casually tossed the can a few yards out on the plain and took his first shot at it. The can clanked hollowly in the great empty plain and spun dizzily through the air like a whirling pinwheel, coming to rest at a considerable distance from us. Tom's second shot sent the can bouncing again. His third shot found home too, despite the hairline calculations he had to make to aim true in that wind. By that time the can was barely visible; only the tiniest gleam of metal distinguished its presence on a patch of dun-colored earth near a scraggly piece of sagebrush bent dead in the wind. I thought Tom's individual shooting meet was over, because nobody could move that can again in a brisk wind at that distance. But Tom did. He moved it twice more, until not a single trace of the shining metal could be seen.

I was scarcely less impressed than the boy and his mother. Though I had seen plenty of fast, accurate Western shooting in my time, none had ever matched this.

I looked at my husband proudly, and saw the shine of admiration in the widow's eyes. I was sure she was thinking along with me that we were safe as long as men like Tom were on the right side of a gun; that if it hadn't been for men like Tom, the West would never have been won and passed on to posterity.

There is no doubt that Tom's facility with a gun saved his life many times. But there is also ample evidence to prove that he never used a gun injudiciously. He never shot to kill when he could shoot to wound. He never shot at all if he could settle a dispute with his fists. And he didn't use his fists if he could settle a difference with words. During his career Tom stopped many a killing, and many a fight from blossoming, simply by talking common sense.

During his picture career he had his own code. He refused to portray himself as a drunk or be shown partaking of hard liquor, and he would never smoke on the screen. His appearances in saloons had to be for the purpose of dealing out justice to a bad man. Respect must be shown for womanhood, even the toughest dance-hall girl. As a hero in pictures he never accepted reward money, but always turned it over to some worthy cause. If the story demanded that he fall in love with a girl, she generally had to be "the ranch owner's daughter" or a schoolteacher.

No matter how quickly Tom had to make decisions—and some of the scrapes he got into called for instantaneous, explosive action—his were always reasoned decisions. When he had time for a real think-through, he could usually come up with a plan that would avoid violence and save lives.

Such an occasion arose when Tom was sheriff of a cattle town in Colorado a few years before our marriage. The town had attracted a small gang of cattle thieves who had pulled some successful rustling jobs. There was no proof against them. But honey always attracts flies. Tom knew the community would be swarming with rustlers when the word spread that cattle could be lifted from the ranges with ease.

Tom had a "thinking session." One day he secretly shot three precise holes through the tops of three surveyors' pegs. Then he waited for the right moment to carry through his plan. It came one day when he spied the rustlers gathered on the plain near the edge of town. He calmly rode his horse out to a spot where he was certain the rustlers could plainly see what he was doing. He dismounted and planted the pegs in the earth. Then he remounted, drew his gun, and made it obvious that he was going to have a bit of target practice. He drew back a few hundred yards and thundered toward the three-peg target at full gallop. He shot at the first peg from his right hand, flipped the gun to his left hand to shoot at the second peg, and took care of the final peg with a flourishing shot behind his back.

Annie Oakley couldn't have placed three precise holes in three small pegs at that distance and that speed of gallop! But the thieves were convinced that Tom had done it. Tom rode calmly back to town and turned to see the thieves examining the pegs with awe. The next morning they were gone.

It was a psychological ruse that worked. Outlaws invariably

respected a sharpshooter, especially a sharpshooting sheriff. Tom avoided a great deal of bloodshed for the entire town that would have inevitably occurred if the rustling had continued.

I didn't know that story, either, on the windy day of our wedding journey, but I already had an inkling that getting to know my husband was going to be a long and involved process.

I couldn't suppress a little shrug of disappointment when we got off the train in Miles City, Montana. What a dreary place to start a honeymoon! For Miles City in 1909 was just beginning to grow out of its swaddling clothes.

Most frontier towns, in their infancy, were unimaginative collections of unpainted frame buildings, the one main street a frozen mass of pock holes in the winter, a sleazy ooze of mud in the spring, and a powdery bed of red dust in the summer. The beauty was not in the towns but in the surrounding country. And there is no other beauty like Western beauty. There are no other colors like Western colors. There are no other skies with the bright, living intensity of Western skies. No other sweeping vistas anywhere else could match the magnitude of the broad avenues Nature has sculptured in the West. When God was handing out the grandeur, he planted much of it in that portion of the country.

Some of the towns, however, were bits of gray bitterness in their grand settings of the richest of Nature's accomplishments. Many were flimsily constructed because the possibility of permanency was only a matter of conjecture. Some of the towns withered and died in their infancy, abandoned to the elements when a mining shaft was depleted or a cattle trail shifted.

Miles City was destined to mature. But it wasn't fashionably grown when Tom and I were there. It looked pretty bleak to me and I remembered that spring would be coming soon in Oklahoma. Spring might not reach Montana for another two or three months.

"Tom," I said, "let's go home. It's so beautiful there now." I laughed. "And I want to show *you* off."

"Home's our next stop," he chuckled. "But we've got a little business here to attend to first."

Miles City was significant to Tom because it was one of the many places he had called home during his Western wanderings. Of course, the whole West was home to Tom. He had put down his stakes and had ridden the range anywhere the bunchgrass grew. In his capacity as a law officer he had helped a dozen communities to struggle out from under the duress of bad elements. When a place was cleaned up, it was time for him to move on, for there were always other communities that needed help. The entire West that emerged after the shambles and conflict was the final product of men like Tom. In a very real sense Tom, and men like him, saved the West for us as surely as the men of our struggling Continental Army saved our country for us.

During his roaming years Tom was a sheriff many times over, a deputy U. S. Marshal, a Texas Ranger, a cowboy, a ranch foreman, and a soldier. For a time he was City Marshal at Dewey, Oklahoma, not more than a hundred miles from our ranch, in the days when I was being teased by my brother and my uncle, and utterly oblivious to the fact that I would one day grow up to marry Tom. He was also special enforcement officer of Indian Territory for a time.

I learned of Tom's military accomplishments when we were guests at Bill Tambler's ranch outside Miles City.

"Seen Teddy lately?" asked Bill.

"Not since he invited us to the White House in 1906," said Tom casually.

I thought that Tom and Bill were having a joke at my expense. So I laughed. Then I realized suddenly that it wasn't a joke.

"Do you mean that you *know* Theodore Roosevelt?" I gasped.

"Sure," said Tom, and prepared to stop right there.

Bill chuckled. "Tom doesn't talk much about those days. Guess he's ashamed of getting his head in the way of that bullet—considering how short the Spanish-American War was."

Tom grinned and said nothing, and I exploded. "Tom Mix, you *tell* me!"

"Well, they needed men," he said laconically. "So I joined the Rough Riders."

Between Tom and Bill I managed to wheedle out the whole story. Tom was eighteen when hostilities broke out. He left school immediately and was in the thick of the affray when Theodore Roosevelt led his Rough Riders in the Battle of San Juan Hill in Cuba, the most severe battle of the ten-week war.

But Tom didn't take his bullet in that battle. It was in a cleanup operation, when they were shaking the Spaniards out of palm trees, that Tom met his first hot sting of lead. A Spanish sharpshooter secreted in some fronds shot Tom. The bullet went through his mouth and out the back of his head. He spent a month in the hospital. But that was only the first of the many close bullet wounds he was to sustain and survive during his career.

Tom next joined the provisional army for service in the Philippines. He ended up in the Boxer Rebellion in China where he sustained a severe chest wound—the second soldier to be wounded in that insurrection—and was so badly hurt that he was sent home and mustered out of service. He was barely twenty years old, but he had already been close to death from war injuries.

When Tom returned to the United States, he took a job breaking wild horses for use by the English in the Boer War. When these horses were loaded on freighters, bound for South Africa, Tom went along too. In South Africa he showed the English what a cowboy could do with a horse, a Western saddle, and a rope; and they were duly impressed. He did very little fighting, however, though he did participate in the siege of Ladysmith, and emerged from the war with a wound in his shoulder and also in one arm to add to his rapidly growing collection.

In the Boer War, too, Tom made his initial appearance in motion pictures, though at a great distance from the lens. An American movie company had sent a unit to Africa to film some of the war's highlights. Tom was a speck in a couple of the scenes.

I remember Tom laughing about that incident during the evening we spent with Bill, and how it led us into a discussion of the films. In 1909 a lot of people thought the motion picture industry had progressed as far as it would ever go; in some quarters it was still being considered a passing fad.

At that time the Western film was beginning to blossom on the screen. Tom said something typically laconic to express his opinion of the pictures he had seen.

"They're not *real* enough," he said. "Just a lot of counterfeit cowboys making fun of the West. They're an insult to the true West!"

He wasn't referring merely to the unauthentic background scenery used in the early two-reelers. He was speaking also of the wild gesticulation and false, exaggerated acting that the "Western" players brought to the screen in those days.

Tom was later to bring the broad, real actions of the Western hero to the screen, probably to a greater degree than any other actor. He banished from the Western film the wild flaying of arms and ridiculous facial distortions that simu-

lated action and emotion in the early Westerns. As a *true*
son of the West he brought to the screen a reflection of the
authentic actions and emotions that had been part of him all
of his life.

On that night the possibility of Tom's becoming a screen
star was the most remote thing from our minds. I was in the
process of wondering where we would settle. Like any other
new bride I was already forming in my mind a picture of the
home Tom and I would share. Before we said good night to
Bill I had built the house, mentally, in the wooded section
of our Oklahoma ranch. On the way back to Miles City I was
thinking: *Just wait until Tom gets a real taste of our ranch.
His itchy feet will stop itching.*

Overlooking the truth in my flush of newlywed happiness,
I suppose I was trying to convince myself that we were going
to settle down. Something that should have been obvious to
me even then was that the chances were nil for us to lead
an ordinary, settled life. For Tom was in no sense an ordinary
man and in no way fitted for a placid, routine life; and the
life we were to lead together was destined to be extraordinary
—one where the joys and the heartbreaks press much harder in
intensity than they do in the smooth way of the settled life.
We were destined to feel the full impact of the joys and the
heartbreaks, together and apart.

On that night the overwhelming future was still ahead of
us. I was dreaming of our home and Tom was busy wondering whether a certain surprise he had for me would be ready
the next day.

It was. He had ordered twin saddles for us from Al Furst-
now, the foremost saddlemaker in the West at that time. The
saddles were exquisite examples of fine craftsmanship, taste-
fully ornamented with just the proper amount of silver work.
Both Tom and I were to use them in the ranch shows we later
appeared in. These were the first ornamented saddles either

of us had owned. They were the forerunners of the huge collection of ornate saddles that Tom was to have at the crest of his movie and circus careers—some of them costing thousands of dollars.

Tom bought me a buckskin skirt and jacket. "Well, this is quite an unusual kind of trousseau!" I laughed.

Tom laughed too and proceeded to buy for himself a pair of batwinged chaparajos stamped with silver. The chaps were obviously for display and not for hard range use. They weren't a bit more practical than my beaded buckskin skirt and jacket were.

Tom must have read my mind. "Don't worry, Olive," he said, "we'll get a lot of use out of these."

To top it all, I discovered Tom's love of diamonds, a passion that was to cost him hundreds of thousands of dollars during later years. But he was considerate enough on this day to make his purchase at a pawn broker's. He bought me a huge diamond and insisted upon waiting until the ring was cut down so that he could put it on my finger.

Finally, when I was utterly exhausted, Tom turned to me with a smile. "Well, how about going home now, Olive?"

3 ∾

Was It Real — or a Movie?

WE WERE HOME FOR A WEEK BEFORE I MENTIONED WHAT was most on my mind, for I wanted to be certain that Tom had time to fall under the spell of our ranch before I brought up the subject of settling down.

Tom had stopped at the ranch briefly before following me to Medora, so briefly, in fact, that he had rather frightened Mother with his reluctance to tell her just why he wanted to see me. Mother had worried over what the dark, silent young man was going to do.

When we arrived home Mother, after a few still moments, succumbed to Tom's charm. He had the glad effect of a Chinook wind on her, and she was soon forgetting how shocked she'd been when Luke returned home with the news of our marriage. She fretted all the time Tom and I were in Miles City, convinced that I had reverted to my impulsive childhood temperament and had flung myself into a marriage with a man I scarcely knew.

This time Tom had spent no more than an hour under our roof before Mother was completely pacified. He treated her like a Queen Mother, and soon she was wondering why we had delayed our marriage so long!

Before he had been at the ranch twenty-four hours he knew the name of every hand we had. He threw himself right into the ranch routine, one with which he was thoroughly familiar after his rich practical experience as cowhand and ranch foreman on so many ranches of the Plains states. In fact, he was so busy working around the place that I became a little irritated.

"This is supposed to be our honeymoon," I reminded him one day.

Tom laughed. "I've got to start getting back into the swing, Olive," he said. "Can't get soft."

Later I was to reflect that the comparatively physically inactive month Tom had spent courting me was the only inactive month he ever spent. Love had slowed him down to a half run, and now love was to be the basis of the future he was planning for us.

Love was the basis of my plan for our future too, a plan that was centered around the ranch and the imaginary house I had already built in the woods. It made me happy that within a week Tom seemed to be in love with the ranch; and that the place was assuredly in love with him.

We rode down to the sawmill on a beautiful morning that I decided was the time to take the plunge. Tom dismounted from Old Blue, a glossy blue-black cowpony that had been his faithful companion through his years of sheriffing, marshaling, spring and fall roundups, and Wild West shows. He swung me down from my horse and we walked hand in hand through the woods. The ash and walnut trees rushed up toward a spotless sky, the lemon-spread sky of the mild Oklahoma winter—another perfect day created for Tom and me alone, I thought as I inhaled the pungent freshness of the countryside.

"This would make a nice spot for our house," I ventured cautiously when we reached a knoll in the woods hung deep with stately sycamores and carpeted in the spring with the bright pink clouds of redbud.

"Now wait a minute, Olive," said Tom.

"Well—we have to live *somewhere*," I raced on.

Tom spoke calmly. "Olive, this is your family's ranch—"

"Well, you're family now."

"It isn't the same," he explained. "We're going to have our own ranch some day, but *I'm* going to get it for us."

I should have known by then that no one handed anything to Tom Mix on a silver platter. He was far too big a man for that. But all I could think of was that *here* we had everything we could ever want. Our ranch was rich—further richened by the discovery of oil on it—and the hard years of building were over. I couldn't understand Tom's wanting to go through a struggle when everything was already set up for us. Dinner was on the table, but Tom wasn't eating.

He took my hand. "Olive, I know how you feel about your home, but you're my life now, and I'm your life. Ever since I was a kid I've wanted my own ranch. It's what I've worked for all along. Now I'll be working for us, for *our* ranch. Understand?"

I did understand.

"Of course," he went on, "if you think you couldn't be happy anywhere but here—well, I guess—"

I stopped him. Of course he was right. But he faltered in his purpose at that moment, because of love for me. I often thought afterward what a disaster it would have been for Tom if I had persuaded him, at that moment when his Achilles' heel was exposed, to settle down in the cloistered little dream world that looked so wonderful to me then. The world would never have seen its greatest cowboy star! But many of the twistings of life depend upon decisions made at vulnerable moments. The world gained because I decided to make what I thought was a personal sacrifice. If I had used Tom's love as a weapon then, my own world might not have fallen apart some years later.

What I did was look toward the lovely woods, swallow hard and say, "All right. *Our own ranch*. How are we going to get our start?"

"Wild West shows," he said. "I've got some letters out now, and an offer's sure to come along. We'll have to work for someone else for a while, but we'll have our own show eventually. That'll make us the money to get the ranch."

I nodded, trying hard to reconcile myself to the idea of living a life of train rides and one-night stands.

I remembered the beaded buckskin skirt and jacket Tom had bought me, and the elaborate chaps he had bought for himself. "We'll have to use them," he said. That meant he intended me to be a part of the show too.

When I pressed the point, he explained: "I thought you might want to. You sit on a horse better'n any woman I know. As for handling a gun—well, I'd sure hate to have you mad at me."

I snuggled up against him, enormously pleased with myself. The thought of the shows suddenly took on a sweet quality. I was envisioning myself as a sort of Annie Oakley riding at Tom's side and performing unheard-of shooting and riding feats before the fascinated eyes of thousands.

Besides, wasn't a woman supposed to do what her husband wanted? So the matter was settled.

"When do you think we'll be starting?"

"You know, Olive," Tom replied, "I used to think there wasn't any greater happiness in the world than just riding the range where a man could feel bigger than anywhere else." He reached for my hand. "But I guess a man can't really feel big until he has something like this."

Any doubts about the impetuosity of my marriage were entirely dispelled at that moment.

During those first weeks of our marriage an event occurred that gives insight into the deep feeling Tom had for animals. An animal was never "dumb" to Tom. He always treated them with kindness and deep respect.

We had ridden to Bartlesville that day to talk with Clay McDonigal, an old friend of Tom's and the champion roper of the world at that time. Clay was making only a brief stopover at Bartlesville; so Tom and I were ready to start back to the ranch by midafternoon.

When we had ridden in at noon we noticed the horse sale in progress at a corral, at the edge of town. On our way home past the corral we saw a man abusing a horse.

The man wasn't sparing the whip as he tried to pull the skittish, frightened horse out of the corral. A couple of bystanders laughed as the horse reared upward in snorting fright and came crashing down, barely missing his abuser. The man angrily cracked the horse's flanks with his whip again.

"I'll show you right now who your master is!" he shouted in fury.

Tom was already off Old Blue. His mouth was set hard as he leaped over the corral fence and dashed toward the man. He reached him just in time to stop him from making a new attack with the whip. The horse stopped skittering and danc-

ing immediately as though he knew someone had come to
help him.

I saw Tom's hand tighten around the horse-abuser's wrist
until the whip fell to the ground.

"That's better," said Tom. "You don't seem to understand
much about horses, Mister."

In those days nothing could gather an audience faster than
the prospect of a brawl. I dismounted quickly. By the time I
reached the corral fence people were coming from all directions.

Tom had been on the horse-abuser so quickly that it took
the man a moment to respond. Then, as his rage mounted, he
reached down for the whip.

But Tom's boot was pressed securely on it.

"I said you don't seem to understand much about horses,
Mister," Tom repeated.

The man's face reddened with anger as he looked at the
snickering crowd gathered to watch his humiliation. He
balled his fists and glared at Tom.

Tom ignored the hot glare. "Horses have feelings," Tom
said. "They don't act contrary unless something scares them,
Mister." He reached down, picked up the whip, and flung it
across the corral. "You don't need a whip to get that horse
out of the corral if you treat it right—"

"Look, I bought this horse," the man said. "I've got a right
to do what I—"

"You're wrong, Mister. You haven't got any right—"

The man's fist shot out at Tom.

"I guess there's no other way to settle this," Tom said as he
took one lightning swing that landed the man in the dust.
The fellow sat there, clutching his jaw in pain and amazement,
as Tom threw a roll of bills down at him. "Guess that'll more
than cover what you paid for the horse."

Tom walked up to the animal, talked quietly into its ear,

patted it gently on its neck, and led it out of the corral. He grinned at me. "Guess the ranch can stand another horse, can't it, Olive?"

I nodded. I couldn't say anything at that moment. I was near tears with admiration for my husband. From the comments the crowd of onlookers was impressed too. They followed us with their eyes as we headed out of town, our new horse walking behind us with the docility of a lamb.

"A horse will respect a man who respects him," Tom said as he glanced back at our new acquisition.

That statement summed up his attitude toward his own animals. He was to own over a hundred horses before his career was finished, many of them recalcitrant under any hands but his own.

I always wrote to Tom's mother regularly. She and Tom's father lived at a tiny hamlet known as "Mix Run," near the city of Dubois, Pennsylvania.

This correspondence started right after we left Medora, when Tom asked me to write his mother and tell her of our marriage. I think one thing he disliked more than anything else was to write letters.

It was through this exchange of letters with his mother that I learned more about his early youth than I had been able to do up to that time. Whenever I brought up the subject of his childhood he would mention a few details and then switch to some topic that had to do with the present or future.

Tom was born in Mix Run in 1880. From what his mother wrote, his schooling had been very sketchy because he was more interested in being with his father who owned a stable in Dubois. It was here that his love of horses began. He almost lived in the saddle, though there were intervals when he would go hunting in the woods or fishing.

In a letter that I have always treasured, his mother told me of an episode that started Tom out in life with a determination to do whatever he set out to do better than anyone else. He entered a bicycle race against several score contestants. But unlike most of them, he trained for the race for months—riding up hill and down dale for miles and miles each day.

After he won the race his mother discovered a piece of paper on the table in his room. On it he had written the words: *"Whatever you do, do it better than anyone else!"*

Tom's mother related how, even at the tender age of ten, he was dreaming of having his own ranch out West and had conceived a brand for his cattle—an *M* with a *T* slanted diagonally across it.

From a picture sent to me it was apparent Tom's mother was a very beautiful woman—very tiny and with big black eyes and black hair.

I learned from her about his association with the notorious Madero.

"I have always prayed and prayed for Tom," she wrote. "Perhaps I was praying for him at the moment he faced that firing squad in Mexico, and maybe that helped. Tom needed money in those days. He was known throughout the West for his great courage. His reputation reached Mexico too, and Francisco Madero heard of him. I guess you remember Madero. He was that famous Mexican bandit chief who was instrumental in fomenting the Mexican Revolution and who later, starting in 1911, served as Mexico's president until he was assassinated in 1913.

"Madero sent an offer to Tom. He would give him five hundred dollars if Tom would come to Mexico and capture certain of Madero's enemies who were hiding in the Sierra Madres. Tom accepted the offer. But he weighed the matter carefully before deciding. He knew that Madero was fighting to win the land for the Mexican peons. It was a good moral cause.

"So Tom went to Mexico, tracked down Madero's enemies,

and delivered them to him. He expected to collect his money and be on his way, but he found a firing squad waiting for him instead. Apparently he had been framed on some trumped-up charge of violating the Mexican military law. Tempers were volatile in those early revolutionary days and trials were short or nonexistent. Tom was saved only by a last-minute confession of treachery by the man who had testified against him."

At last Tom received the letter he had been waiting for. It was an invitation to join the Widerman Wild West Show in Amarillo, Texas. I knew right away that this was it. Our peaceful days at the ranch were over.

"A small show," said Tom, "but it'll give us some experience so we can start our own show later on."

With considerable misgivings I consented to go along with Tom's desire to sign up for the show. We caught the next train to Amarillo.

On the train I asked Tom how he happened to get into show business. It was another instance of dragging information out of my "man of mystery."

"I worked for a fellow in Mexico," Tom replied. I didn't tell him that I knew that the "fellow" was Madero, through the letter I had received from his mother.

"With the money I earned," Tom went on, "I bought three new horses and teamed them with Old Blue. After a little training I had them dancing in the streets of El Paso." He laughed. "I also did a few rope tricks in the act, but the reception wasn't exactly overwhelming. Just about the time we were ready to starve, I got an offer to join a regular show.

"But what made you even want to go into the business?" I persisted.

"I guess I got the seed planted in me when I was about ten and went to El Paso to watch Bill Cody's show pass through town on the train. I thought there wasn't anyone bigger on earth than Buffalo Bill."

The very next year, in 1910, Colonel Cody was to take full recognition of the boy who had so eagerly watched his entourage pass through El Paso twenty years before. Tom was approached by the owners of Colonel Cody's show with a publicity scheme designed to enhance Tom's future and further line the wallets of the show's owners. It was proposed that Tom take the name of Cody and pose as Buffalo Bill's son, to be his understudy and successor.

Tom turned the offer down flat, despite the fact that he wasn't really secure in his fledgling movie career at that point. It wasn't only that Tom was too proud of his own name and heritage to consider changing it, it was also that his honesty prevented him from entering into anything that smacked of deception, despite the rich monetary rewards it might bring.

"These ranch shows are just as important as cleaning up a band of rustlers," Tom said to me that day on the train. "The old ways are going fast. We've got to keep on showing people what they were."

I understood what he meant. The West was becoming civilized and the possibility of death or violence lurking at every corner had diminished. The skills employed in averting death—the expert markmanship, the hard riding—were passing into decay from non-use.

Foremost in Tom's mind, far above the desire to make money, was his anxiety to show the public what the winning of the West really meant. It was his wish to preserve the old ways, to display them and to communicate their meaning. He offered himself to the public as a genuine example of a way of life.

"Anyway," Tom said as he held my hand on that train ride to Amarillo, "if things go right this season maybe we'll make enough to start out with a little patch of land next year." He looked dreamily out the window at the flat, burnished prairie.

The next year was to mean much more than a small "patch of land" to us, but at that moment 1910 looked awfully far away to me.

When we arrived at Amarillo I found it to be a dry, dusty town swarming with cowboys, ranchers, and gamblers. The town had had its beginning in a collection of hide huts huddled forlornly on the bare prairie in the late eighties. Eventually it grew to become the commercial center of the Texas Panhandle.

Tom took me straight to the hotel where he intended to talk to Mr. Widerman about including me in the show. I waited in the lobby while Tom talked business with Mr. Widerman in the bar.

Amarillo was still short on women in those days. My presence in the lobby of the hotel was sufficient to arouse some unsolicited stares from a tall man sitting across from me. The more I turned my eyes away from him, the more I felt his steady gaze on me. I'd been told plenty of times that I was a "mighty pretty little thing," but somehow it had never affected me in the least. I was never the overly romantic type and neither did I spend hours staring at myself in a mirror, with curlers or tweezers. But one thing I hated was to have any man look at me as though mentally undressing me.

This man's stare was not a nice stare despite the fact that he was dressed like a gentleman. His clothes told me he was an Easterner and the fact that his gun belt did not rest easily on him told me he hadn't been here long. I judged that he was probably a gambler or land speculator who had stopped here to make a quick killing.

No matter what else he was, he was obviously lonely. The stares continued.

Finally I couldn't stand it any longer. "There's the window,

Mister," I said, "why don't you look out?" I flashed my wedding ring at him, but that didn't seem to make any difference.

The man got up and walked toward me, grinning apishly. "Why don't we take a walk—"

He didn't finish because Tom came in at that moment, Mr. Widerman following at his heels.

Tom didn't waste time with words on this occasion. He walked up to the intruder and wrenched the gun out of the man's holster and flung it across the lobby. Then he turned the man around, seized him by the seat of his pants, and pranced him to the door where he bounced him resoundingly into the street.

Tom came back laughing. "Can't say I blame the guy for trying," he said to me, his eyes twinkling.

He had talked Mr. Widerman into including me in the show's program; so I had my chance to start wearing the buckskin skirt and jacket Tom had bought for me in Miles City.

The show was small, but we played to capacity crowds everywhere we went. I did some riding tricks and some target shooting at fast gallop, but mostly played as background to Tom, as did everyone else in the show.

Tom wasn't officially designated as the star of the show, but it was obvious from the very first that the entire exhibition revolved around him. The moment he came tearing into the arena on Old Blue, his energy and fire seemed to reach out and seize the spectators. They sat in an indrawn hush as he performed his elaborate riding tricks, leaping on and off Old Blue with the ease and agility and speed of a jaguar as the horse encircled the arena. He somersaulted backward to a following horse, too; and tight-legged around Old Blue's belly he hung precariously at side angle, his face so close to the ground that it seemed certain that it was being scraped raw as Old Blue raced around the ring. Tom performed his complex display of agile body movements with a precision and grace that would have put a professional acrobat to shame. Sometimes, in the blur of maddening speed, it was as though he and the horse were one.

The audience was dazzled. Years later audiences a hundred times the size of these were to be enchanted by Tom's fine horsemanship in the really big circuses, including his own.

He also did a solo lariat act in the Widerman show. Twirling the lariat, making it respond like a great long arm, looks remarkably easy, but is in fact extremely difficult. Somersaulting off a horse looks easy too, but it is not.

His dexterity with the lariat came from years of practice—just as his superlative horsemanship and unerring aim with the gun were the rewards of years of experience. Tom eschewed the use of the forty-foot lariat, which had a roping reach of only twenty-five feet. He gave the spectators a much better display of skill by using a sixty-foot rope with a reach of forty feet. Tom spun the rope to his exact wishes, just as though it were a breathing animal responding to its master's commands.

Notwithstanding Tom's glowing performance, it was still a small show and a far cry from the extravaganzas Tom was to star in under the big top in later years. However, he was radiant from being back in the harness again, and although I disliked spending half my time on trains and the other half in hotel rooms, I was happy because my husband was happy.

The show hit Kansas City when Will Rogers was playing the Orpheum there. Will had been on the vaudeville circuits since 1905, when he got his big chance with his lassoing act at Hammerstein's Roof Garden in New York City.

Will, Tom and I had dinner together to celebrate our reunion.

"You know," said Will in that inimitable drawl of his, "I had a big feeling back at the St. Louis Fair that something was going to happen to you two one day."

"Well, it sure did, didn't it?" Tom said.

Later that evening Will said to me: "Tom's a real big man, Olive. But he's going to be a whole lot bigger before he's finished." He smiled at me. "Especially with you helping him along."

As things turned out, both Tom and Will were destined to become the biggest of men in their fields. By 1914 Will was appearing in the Ziegfeld Follies, which gave him his final boost to stardom, a high perch he was to hold until his death in 1935 in an airplane crash. As for Tom, his zooming rise to stardom paralleled Will's closely in point of time. It seemed symbolic that the two old friends reached their zenith of fame and accomplishment almost simultaneously.

We hated saying good bye to Will that night, but our itinerary called for a move to Napa, Idaho, for the next playing date.

We never got there.

Tom had told me that he was going to ask Mr. Widerman's nephew, who had taken over management of the show in the owner's absence, to raise our pay. We weren't making much money, considering the important part Tom played in the show, and we hadn't been able to save much for that "patch of land" Tom was always dreaming about.

During a stopover in Denver, Tom stepped outside on the platform with young Widerman to talk over the matter. I watched and listened through the open window.

Young Widerman was an impetuous man with a gun. He knew that without Tom he would have no show, but he was still reluctant to pay Tom his due for the fine job he was doing.

They entered into a heated argument and finally I saw Widerman make a move toward his gun holster. Tom was unarmed.

"Drop that hand, Mister," I called out through the train

window. I was holding a .45 and was glad that this was one time I could help Tom.

Widerman looked over at me, whitened, and dropped his hand.

"Come on, get off the train, Olive," called out Tom.

When I got off Widerman, who had come to his senses, was trying to make Tom reconsider. Tom kept saying no. He wouldn't work for or with a man he didn't respect; and Widerman had completely lost his respect. Still protesting, Widerman finally got back on the train and continued on with the troupe.

As we stood on the platform watching the train disappear into the night with the usual puffing and belching of clouds of steam that went with railroad engines at that time, Tom smiled. "Well, Olive, I guess we're on our own."

I nodded and returned his smile. I knew we'd get there.

We went into the Union Depot to get a hack to take us to a hotel. We were both too tired to think about the future, but I'll admit I was happy for there seemed to be no other move than to return to the ranch in Oklahoma.

This dream of mine was to last only a few moments, for hardly had we stepped into the depot and started looking around when a tall, wiry young man came up to us. He grinned and extended his hand to Tom.

"Well, I'll be! Tom Mix!"

Tom's face lighted up. "Charlie Tipton!" he exclaimed. "What in heck are you doing here?"

"I might ask you the same question," said Charlie. He turned to me questioningly.

"My wife Olive," introduced Tom.

Charlie shook hands with me. There was a twinkle in his eyes. "Never thought any woman could hog-tie Tom," he said, "but I can see, ma'am, that it wouldn't be hard for you to do it."

I laughed. "Can't you teach Tom to pay compliments like that?"

"Don't you go spoiling her," warned Tom. "But anyway, Charlie, what are you doing here?"

"Waiting for the next train to Seattle," Charlie told him. "There's some doings up at the West Washington Fair Grounds in about three weeks. Thought I might line up something for myself up there." Charlie Tipton was one of the top riders of the West. In 1908 he had won several events in the Cheyenne Frontier Days Celebration.

Tom turned to me. "Remember my ambition about havin' our own show, Olive? I reckon this might be it. The Fair Grounds up there would be a fine spot to open up."

The result was that before the train arrived to take us to Seattle, Tom and Charlie Tipton were partners in some nebulous Wild West show to be formed in Seattle.

I told Tom that I was dead tired and would take a nap on one of the benches. He had suggested going to a nearby bar to get a glass of beer.

Tom gave me some money to buy the tickets and he and Charlie left the depot.

It was going to be an hour before the Seattle train would be made up, so I relaxed on the bench until the caller announced that the train was ready. I boarded the train to continue my sleep, naturally thinking Tom and Charlie would get on too and look for me.

Suddenly I awoke and looked around. The train was moving, but there was no sign of Tom and Charlie. I made a tour of the coaches and questioned the conductor. They were not on the train.

At the next station stop the conductor contacted the Denver station and told me that Tom and Charlie would be coming on the next train and that I was to wait at the Seattle depot.

When later Tom and Charlie joined me, Tom had a hang-dog look. "Guess we just got to talking," he said, "and forgot about train time."

"And I guess you had more than one glass of beer," I retorted. I couldn't help laughing.

Charlie, Tom and I scoured the city of Seattle in an effort to find talent for our forthcoming Wild West show to open at the fair grounds. The weather had been terrible, full of torrential rains, and no one was at all certain that the Fair would draw crowds.

I took a number of looks at the gloomy skies and was ready again to say, "Let's go home." But Tom ran into an old friend by the name of Ezra Black, a former rancher Tom had worked for in Montana. He was now a Washington lumber dealer, and a rich man. When he heard about the show he said he'd like to invest some money in it. This made me feel a little bit better, as I didn't have much faith in the venture anyway.

We had nine days to organize and rehearse a show that, when it was finished, included a troupe of sixty-five persons. It was a do-or-die venture, and if I had had time to stop to look at it with an objective eye I'm sure I would have gone down with a gasp of defeat.

Tom kept us going through those almost sleepless days and nights of grind. His nerves must have been frayed, too, but his smile never left his face. People, of course, just keep right on going when they have a rock of confidence to look at for inspiration, so we all just kept plugging away during the endless rehearsals.

Tom's gentle but firm managing hand had everything in order by the time the opening performance came up.

The Tom Mix Wild West Show opened in the midst of a heartless downpour. The Western Washington Fair Grounds was a tarry ooze from previous rains, and new downpours kept large numbers of persons away from the place. We opened to a half-empty house the first day.

The spectators cheered the show. It was an excellent exhibition despite the fact that it had been put together with such frantic haste.

Tom did all the riding, shooting and roping tricks he'd brought down the house with in the Widerman show. Charlie performed the riding stunts that had made him a champion rider of the West. And Tom and Charlie together put on the only act of the show that had a non-Western flavor to it. Tom had conceived the idea that a joust might add variety; so he and Charlie, at the high point of the show, mounted horses at opposite ends of the tent and hurtled toward each other with long blunt-ended poles, just as knights had done in the jousting contests of the Age of Chivalry in England.

Of course one of them was always knocked off his horse by the other's pole. My heart always drummed during this act, even though I knew that both Tom and Charlie wore heavy armor. It was an act ripe with danger, and any miscalculation with the pole could have sent either of them to the hospital. But Tom was right about the freshness of the act. It stole the show.

We didn't stop there. In an effort to add real spectacle to the show, we employed forty Blackfoot Indians to engage in mock but terribly real-looking battle with the other twenty-five members of our troupe. The Indian wars had been over for twenty years, but audiences still thrilled to see them re-created.

The show really contained a great part of the breath of early Western life. There was a stagecoach act in which the Indians attacked and were repulsed by Tom and Charlie. And there was emphasis on the cowboy's role in Tom's bull-dogging act.

Bulldogging is another feat that looks easy but is not. You bulldog a running steer by jumping off your horse, gripping the steer's neck and horns, and twisting its neck until the steer loses balance and falls. It takes precision timing and a great deal of strength to accomplish this trick, and the results are unpredictable. But Tom brought down the steer with each attempt. A Seattle newspaper sent out a photographer to take his picture doing his bulldogging. The picture appeared with the caption: TOM MIX—WORLD'S CHAMPION BULL-DOGGER.

I thought this publicity would be a stimulant to business. But it wasn't. It just kept on raining.

"Don't worry, Olive," Tom said. He still had that smile of confidence fastened on. "We'll come out of this all right."

I wasn't so sure. And my spirits plunged a little farther down with each passing hour of rain. So I wasn't in a very good humor when a very lovesick girl showed up to shower her affection on Tom.

The girl was a prototype of the feminine fans that were, in addition to his juvenile fans, to adore Tom in the idol age of the screen a few years later. The girl had seen Tom in the show the night before and had immediately fallen in love with him.

She sneaked into the tent the next morning when Tom was holding a special rehearsal of the quadrille performers. Tom was a perfectionist, and he hadn't been satisfied with the quadrille routine that was performed on horseback.

He said, "If you give the people something that's less perfect than you can make it, you're not giving them their money's worth."

So Tom was busy getting the quadrille routine perfected that morning. This type of dancing on horseback was related to the elaborate ballet on horseback which became so popular in the big circuses of later years.

I danced into the tent after the rehearsal broke up, just at the moment the girl came out of her watching place and advanced toward Tom. She couldn't have been more than sixteen or seventeen, but her stride held the firmness of a woman intent upon her purpose.

"You're wonderful!" she gasped to Tom.

Tom saw me then, standing rigid with anger at the rear of the tent. Every nerve exploded in me when Tom grinned and—to vex me—said to the titian-haired girl, "Well, it's nice of you to say that."

The girl beamed. "Oh, you like me *already*, don't you?" she squealed. "I *knew* you would. I wanted to stay and meet you right after the show last night—but Mother wouldn't let me. And I had to sneak out this morning to come here—"

She raced on breathlessly while I advanced toward them. I think I got there just about the moment she was planning to fling herself at Tom and hug him.

Tom said, "This is my wife."

The face that was rosy with excitement suddenly blanched. "You mean you're *married?*" the girl gasped.

"He's *real* married," I said.

I took the girl's arm and led her right out of the tent. I was much more gentle with her than Tom had been with the man who'd been overattentive to me in Amarillo, but I wasn't feeling exactly friendly toward her, and I wasn't disappointed to see her disappear forlornly around the corner. When I returned, Tom was convulsed. I finally laughed too. With all the tension of the show growing in us like fungus, we needed something to laugh at.

If my nerves had not been upended, I wouldn't have dealt with the girl so peremptorily. Already, in our few months of marriage, I had seen many girls look at Tom with loving eyes. Many more of them were to take long looks at him in the future. I soon learned there was nothing to worry about. Tom reserved his long looks for me alone.

With only two days left to show a profit or loss, we made a

tally of our books. The picture was very bleak, though we had made enough to pay our performers and to return most of Mr. Black's investment. Tom insisted on this, although Black was a rich man and had taken a gamble along with us. Tom said, "When I take in a partner who puts up money, I like to see him get it back."

That evening we had a good turnout for the show. Though the skies glowered all day, the rain held off. Right as the show ended, however, the ominous thumping started in the heavens. The audience and performers hurried out to avoid the cloudburst that was sure to come.

The fair grounds emptied rapidly that evening, but Tom and I stayed on at the tent to tabulate the box-office receipts, counting the money by lantern light. Maybe it was our fatigue and our breathless eagerness to see how much we'd taken in that evening that caused us to be careless. Anyhow, we didn't have a gun anywhere near us when three men holding guns burst in on us.

The tallest one seemed to be the leader. "Won't be no trouble if you hand over that money quietlike," he declared.

It was three against two and, besides, Tom and I were weaponless.

"Give them the money," I told him. "It's no use."

"Sure, I'll give it to them," Tom said through clenched teeth. Simultaneously his boot went up like a released arrow. The leader cried out in pain as Tom's boot caught his gun wrist and sent the gun hurtling into the air. I reached immediately for the lantern and doused it just as two shots rang out. I was crying and praying at the same time, hoping against hope that neither of the robbers' bullets had found Tom. It seemed a futile hope, though, for they were almost on top of Tom when they fired.

But when I heard chairs fold up like accordions as bodies fell on them, I knew Tom was still in the fight. I controlled my hysteria and tried to get in close enough to help. I could see almost nothing. There is nothing more terrifying than a fight in darkness. Every sound was magnified a thousand times. I kept thinking that every groan, every cry of pain, was Tom's. I flinched with every crack of a fist, for I was certain that Tom was being beaten to death by the robbers. I screamed and kept on screaming but no one came, for our part of the fair grounds had been deserted for at least a half-hour.

When a body crashed near me, I saw it was one of the robbers. As he rose to renew his attack on Tom, who was made all the more vulnerable by the white show outfit he was wearing, I brought a folding chair down on his head with every ounce of strength I could muster. That put him out of the fight for good.

There were still two more. They kept lashing at Tom like octopus' tentacles and Tom kept lashing back. One robber attacked him from the front while the other simultaneously came at him from the rear. I couldn't get close to either of them, though I had another chair ready to bring crashing down if the opportunity arose.

I wondered if it would ever end; it seemed as though we had been swirling in a black morass for hours.

It did end, and quite abruptly. Tom flung himself on the leader and smashed him to the ground. Though the other robber was thumping on Tom from behind, the leader was rendered unconscious.

That was enough for the back-clinger. He ran. He got through the tent exit and was quite a way down the road by the time Tom found one of the guns on the ground and went after him. Tom yelled at the robber to stop; but the man declined to return willingly to the scene of his torture. Tom fired and hit him in the leg. In a fitting climax to our tempestuous evening, the cloudburst broke in all its fury as Tom dragged his limping victim back to the tent.

With the lantern on again I was able to see, and I was shocked to discover how badly Tom was injured. His face was caked with drying blood. Amazingly he had fought the entire battle of flailing fists with a deep bullet wound scorching his hand. Even this bad injury didn't keep him out of the final performance of the show the next day. Fortunately, his gun and roping hand had escaped.

Tom and I tied the robbers, intending to hand them over to the police. But before we left I picked up every last dollar of the box-office receipts. With the impact of a cyclone the fight had picked up the money in its vortex and had scattered it all over the tent.

After the robbers were delivered and Tom's wounds had been dressed we returned to our hotel room and I finally had time to take stock of everything that had happened.

"Tom, you could have been killed," I said palely. I was shaking. I could feel my heart turning over in me.

Tom took my hand and pressed it. "I wasn't killed. And you weren't hurt. That's what's important."

"But taking that chance—"

"I had to take it, Olive," Tom said. Then he dropped off to sleep from sheer exhaustion.

I lay awake for a long time. If Tom and I were settled down on the ranch, I thought, things like this wouldn't happen. I cried myself to sleep.

The Fair ended the next day in an explosion of rain. The final performance brought in enough money to square our accounts. The weather had been against us all along, but there was one sweet side to the picture: we had put on a good show and Tom had proved his competence as an impresario and showman. We had accomplished something.

Nevertheless I was discouraged. The excitement of the battle in the tent and my all but sleepless night, not to mention the fatiguing business of packing up the show, had left me exhausted and short-tempered. Somehow I felt I just couldn't face going through it all again. I blew up.

Tom sighed. "I don't blame you for feeling that way, Olive. I've put you through a lot the last couple of months. I know it hasn't been much fun for you—all this work and insecurity—"

I felt bitterly ashamed of myself. Here I was whining and ready to give up again, and had not even given him a fair chance to show what he could really do.

"I don't really want to go home." My shame drove me to say that.

But we were never destined to go home at that time, for a few days later a letter came to me from an old friend of our family's, Will Dickey. He had been putting on a show and touring the country. Apparently from what he wrote he was now deeply interested in motion pictures, and was under contract to the Selig Polyscope Company in Chicago. It was the biggest picture company in the business at that time.

Will Dickey knew about Tom and wanted me to see if I couldn't persuade him to come to Flemington, Missouri, and act in some new Western pictures they were going to make.

I didn't know how Tom would take the idea of getting out of show business to go into moving pictures, about which he knew absolutely nothing. To my surprise he agreed enthusiastically.

"And we'll stop over in Cheyenne for the Frontier Days celebration," he announced. "Maybe I can pick up some prize money there."

Cheyenne, Wyoming, in those days was a wild and woolly city. Aside from being a terminal point for three railroads, it also boasted a United States Army fort—Fort Russell, where Negro recruits were trained. Cheyenne boasted probably one of the biggest red-light districts in the entire West, with many colored prostitutes to take care of "Army requirements." On the other hand it had some flourishing manufacturing plants and was the first city in the United States to be lighted by electricity.

Tom and I registered at the Plains Hotel, which was the outstanding one in the city. The rooms were immense and it seemed as if we had moved into a ballroom. We were lucky to get a room at all, however, as the city was filled with visitors who had arrived for the big celebration and rodeo. In those days the celebration of Frontier Days was still being held on a prairie north of town and the events consumed only a day or two of time. It has since expanded to an elaborate one-week fiesta and attracts thirty or forty thousand outside spectators.

Nowadays the tide of fiesta spirit sweeps into Cheyenne weeks before the actual celebration begins, when the citizens start dressing in the colorful costumes of their pioneer forebears. A large contingent of Sioux Indians comes in from a Dakota reservation to demonstrate tribal rites. There are color-splashed parades and a huge pageant featuring the development of transportation in America. These elaborate *hors d'oeuvres* precede the daily events, which include calf roping, bulldogging, bronco- and steer-riding, the cowgirls' relay race, the Indian squaw race, the cowboys' pony race, wild horse races, and military maneuvers.

In 1909 there were no *hors d'oeuvres*, but the basic structure of the contests of skill was much the same as it is now.

Tom had put his name down for the calf-roping contest and the bronco-busting contest. The prize money for the former was small, but the prize for the bronco contest was one hundred dollars.

Tom got Number 1 in the drawing for riders who would participate in the first day's events. His horse was to be a bronco named Sabile.

Clayton Banks, who was staying at the Plains Hotel, had won first money the year before so I approached him, introduced myself and asked:

"What kind of horse is this Sabile?"

"Mrs. Mix, he's the crookedest horse in the whole world!"

I didn't tell him that Tom made a specialty of overcoming "crooked horses." They are the ones that turn and twist with savage intent to throw their rider.

Being lucky to get a box seat in the grandstand, I found myself in an excellent viewing position. There was only one other occupant of the box, the manager of the Plains Hotel. I didn't know him, but I recognized him from having seen him at the hotel.

In the next box was seated Charlie Irwin who put on the show, a massive man weighing close to three hundred pounds.

It was nearing time for the bronco-busting contest. Charlie Irwin had been studying the program. He turned around and exclaimed, "I'll bet five hundred dollars that this boy from Oklahoma doesn't ride Sabile three jumps!"

I dug into my "grouch bag," which (like most women in those days) I carried in the bosom of my dress. Taking out five one-hundred-dollar bills, I looked over at Charlie Irwin and said, "I'll take that bet, Mr. Irwin!"

The big man looked at me in surprise. He did not know that the rider of Sabile was my husband.

"Who are you?" he demanded gruffly.

"Don't matter who I am. I've got five hundred dollars to cover that bet. Put up or shut up."

He kept looking at me without speaking.

Turning to the manager of the hotel, I said, "Would you mind holding the stakes, Mr. Baker?"

"If Mr. Irwin is serious, I'll be delighted," said Mr. Baker with a smile.

Charlie Irwin passed over a five-hundred-dollar bill and Mr. Baker took it and my five hundreds. He winked at me as he did so. Evidently he knew that I was Tom's wife.

Although I had confidence Tom would win, I was a little shaky as I watched them blindfold Sabile in front of the grandstand and saw Tom standing there with his usual calm expression. In those days there were no chutes to put the horses in prior to riding them.

From the first moment Tom dropped on that horse it looked as though the contest would go strictly against him. Tom tightlegged the horse at once and attached his hand to the buckstrap like iron to a magnet. But the horse went into an immediate frenzy in its twisting attempts to unfasten from its back what it considered to be a loathsome burden. It reared and plunged and shook and bounced and danced; and the centrifugal force alone would have hurled any but the most extraordinary rider from the saddle.

But Tom clung on under the terrific impact of the jolts and by the time he finished the mile stretch the horse was running and not bucking.

When it was over I smiled over at Charlie Irwin as Mr. Baker passed over the thousand dollars—my five hundred and the winnings.

"It was worth it," remarked Charlie Irwin. "I never thought the guy could do it!"

The next day I had a perverse desire to show Charlie Irwin that I was "somebody" and that Tom Mix was my husband; also that I would still eat if Tom didn't win the prize money. For on that very morning I had received my royalty check from the government. While Tom and I had been wandering around the country oil had been discovered on our ranch land, and the government was required to pay royalties on land deeded to the Indians, in the event of oil discoveries. I had already signed a voucher for the money due to me in

Seattle and sent it on to Washington with instructions to mail my check to the Plains Hotel in Cheyenne.

Armed with the check, I called on Charlie Irwin at the rodeo headquarters. "Mr. Irwin, I wonder if you would mind endorsing a check for me?"

He glowered down at me. "I wouldn't endorse a check for nobody."

This was what I expected. I held the check under his nose.

He looked at it. "You don't need no endorsement on this— it's a Treasury check!"

We got to talking and I told him I was Tom's wife. This was the start of a friendship that lasted throughout the years. He was a bluff man, but when you got to know him he was big at heart. More than one impoverished family owed their existence to his generosity.

The celebration was over and it was time for us to fulfill our engagement with Will Dickey and the Selig Polyscope Company.

4 ～

The Range Rider

TOM'S FIRST FILM FOR THE SELIG COMPANY WAS FIT-tingly titled *The Range Rider*.

In 1909 the motion picture business was just emerging from a series of tribulations that would have left the ordinary infant enterprise dying on its feet. But the motion picture industry, not being an ordinary one and being made up of a group of ferociously determined people, had come to stay.

A lot had happened since 1895, when Mr. Edison revealed the kinetoscope to the public for the first time. This was a queer-looking wooden cabinet into which one could peer through a slit in the top and see the photographic phenomenon of a child laughing in full motion. It was a sensation. Some people said it was done with mirrors, and some even had an idea there were dwarfs secreted in the cabinet.

When it was proved that these conjectures were wrong, it was said that the peep show couldn't develop into anything bigger, that it was a mere entertainment novelty that would pass into oblivion once the first flavor had been dissipated. Nevertheless, crowds flocked to those first peep shows in New York City.

And people entered into the motion picture business too. By 1900 an astonishing number of companies had been formed, including many one-man organizations. The first years were the most anguished ones in the baby movie industry. There were patent wars and talent stealing and wild experiments. Fortunes made in a week were lost in a day. Only the sturdiest and staunchest of the producers survived the chaos.

But the industry grew with Gulliver strides. People flocked to the tents and the nickelodeons and the music halls where the early films were shown. The "incident" film, where the audience was held in awe simply by seeing something as inconsequential as a man entering and leaving a house with nothing else happening, gave way to a unanimous demand for real stories after *The Great Train Robbery* stunned the public in 1903. Films grew and sharpened and some were even one half-hour long. The two-reel plotted film came into being. In 1909 it seemed impossible that the film could go much further; technically, the movies were already supposed to be at their zenith.

The Range Rider was to be a realistic portrayal of Western life. It was to be filmed entirely in Missouri against a natural outdoor background; and the interior scenes were to be made in specially constructed buildings. None of the painted and obviously phony backdrops of the early days were to be used.

"It's an important picture," the director told us when we arrived at the ranch near Flemington, Missouri, where the company had gathered to make the picture. "Selig has made more money on Westerns than on any other type of picture,

and we're going to concentrate almost exclusively on them
from now on. This one will be our biggest so far."

The star stystem was not established at that time. It would
take Mary Pickford and Charles Chaplin to make a permanent
entrenchment in that direction. But Selig had already created
the first real cowboy star of America in the person of Bronco
Billy, known off-screen as George Anderson. Bronco Billy had
recently left Selig to start his own producing company.

It is true that the Selig people were striving for better pictures. And they sensed that Tom could bring to the screen,
even in that first two-reeler, the broad *real* gestures and actions of the Western hero. All that was necessary was for him
to be natural, for everything they required of him was already his owing to his years of experience.

He had that extra special thing, too, that has never quite
adequately been defined, that quality that makes the difference between being a star and not being a star. It was the same
in 1909 as it is now in that respect.

Tom's leading lady in *The Range Rider* was Myrtle Steadman. William V. Mong played the part of the villain.

For there had to be a villain. Audiences would have been
terribly disappointed if that black unsavory character weren't
around to trip up the hero in everything he tried to do. The
plots of Western films were already pretty well formulated.
The hero was "Goodness" and the villain was "Evil" and the
spotless heroine was the "Reward of the Good." What distinguished each picture a little form every other one was the obstacles the hero had to overcome to get his reward. The obstacles were always different.

Imagination flowed freely in the creation of those films. But
as Tom said: "The real truth is basically there, because Good
always did eventually overcome Evil in the real winning of
the West."

The picture took almost a month to make, a phenomenal period of time to spend in shooting a two-reeler. Some movies were made in a day, and certainly very few of them were in production more than a week.

Much attention to detail was given to *The Range Rider*. The script was changed almost daily in accordance with suggestions from Tom. Written continuities for films at that time were nothing like the elaborate scripts of today; in some instances the director had no more than an outline of the story and figured out his camera shots as he went along. A few directors disdained having a script at all, and worked out all the sequences mentally. Probably in their wildest dreams they would never have envisioned a writer taking eight months to a year to write a "shooting script."

Otis Turner was genuinely pleased with Tom. "It's good to have a man doing this who's *lived* the things we're trying to get across in this picture," he said.

Otis was also pleased that he had to hire no double to perform the difficult stunts that audiences had come to demand. Moviegoers weren't exactly jaded from the old tricks by then; but they were always looking for something newer and more harrowing than the last ones they had seen, something that could really make them grip the theater benches in vicarious terror.

Tom used no double for any of the scenes of *The Range Rider*. And he used no double in any of his later pictures when his stunts, if anything, became even more difficult and complex. This is amazing when you consider that his motion picture career covered a span of more than a quarter of a century. He made a total of around 375 pictures.

Over the years he preserved his marvelous physical stamina by constant and meticulous care of his body. He never for a moment allowed his physical fitness to sag. When he wasn't

active before the cameras he devoted his days to riding and to
target practice and acrobatic stunts. He watched his weight
carefully; it did not vary two pounds from year to year.

Some of Tom's screen stunts were leaping on and off the
backs of racing horses, jumping on trains going by at maddening speed, dragging along the ground by the stirrup, leaping
over impossibly wide and terribly genuine chasms, and jumping on horseback from horrendous heights. These were only
the basic stunts. There were many others, and many varia-
tions.

His refusal to use a double landed him in the hospital many
many times over the years. His shattered bones in his movie
days exceeded many times over his score of bullet wounds and
bodily injuries from his soldiering and sheriffing days. But he
wouldn't even listen in later years to suggestions that he use a
double for some of the seemingly impossible stunts he had
designed for his films. Such suggestions grated against his
basic honesty.

"The public pays to see the genuine article," he said. "Well,
they're not going to get anything phony from me."

He would no more have thought of cheating his fans than he
would have thought of cheating his family or friends. Truth
was the quality Tom lived by all his life.

When *The Range Rider* was wrapped up, we still weren't
aware that Tom would ever make another film.

Otis Turner and Will Dickey thought otherwise.

"When Chicago sees this, they'll be breathing down your
neck," Will Dickey laughed. "I wish I had authority to sign
you to a contract right now, but I don't have it. Just let me
know where we can find you."

"If you want us, we'll be at Medora, North Dakota," Tom
told him. He had promised Bill McCarty that he would come
up and help with the fall roundup, and I was to have a chance
to visit Nels and Katrine again.

Tom really didn't think Selig would want him. Neither did
I. It was apparent that Will Dickey was a high-pedestal man
with Selig and surely he must have authority to give contracts.
No doubt he was trying to shuffle us off in a nice way.

I didn't know that motion picture contracts were still comparatively rare in those days. Only the established players had
them. Picture companies wouldn't even have tied themselves
with these had there not been a rash of "player stealing"
among the various companies in the last few years. Contracts
came into being when the public began taking a liking to a
particular face or personality.

We proceeded contractless to Medora.

There was a wonderful reunion with Nels and Katrine. It
took me a week to tell them everything that had happened to
Tom and me in the three-quarters of a year that we'd been
married. It was only then, when I relived it all with Nels and
Katrine, that I realized how fast time had flown for Tom and
me. How many episodes we had been through in a few short
months!

Now I was to feel my first pang of loneliness at being separated from Tom. For the cattle roundup was strictly a man's
job.

There were two roundups a year: one in the spring and one
in the fall. The purpose of the roundup was to brand ownership marks on calves that had been born since the last roundup and to single out certain of the matured stock for shipment
to market.

In between roundups the cattle roamed freely on the
ranges and proceeded to fatten themselves up for marketing.
It was miraculous that cattle could survive, let alone grow fat,
on the arid tablelands of the Plains states. It would seem that
the cattle-raising industry would be more logically located in
the East, with its hills and fields of thick rich grass.

This would be the case were it not for the grama grass and

buffalo grass, known in combination as bunchgrass, which grows in scattered bunches throughout the Plains states. This is the rich fodder that nature provides to support the vast cattle industry. It grows on the ranges only in the late spring and early summer, then dries on its stalk and is cured by the sun. In this dried, cured form the grass is more nutritious for cattle than any kind of fresh grass known. With a stomachful of this fodder cattle can make journeys of hundreds of miles without a bit of supplementary food.

The building of the cattle industry in the West rested on two factors: the vast amount of grazing land available and the highly nutritive matting of bunchgrass that nature provided free of charge. And cattle raising, more than any other contributing factor, gave the West its particular flavor, its real difference from everything else and everywhere else. The byproduct, the cowboy, still is the major symbol of Western life, the colorful individual who gives the Old and the New West its distinctive flavor. The pioneer, the Indian, the gunman, and the miner all played major roles in the seething drama underlying the forming of the West, but the cowboy, in his simplicity and roughness and life of hardship, was to survive all the others as the leading man of the drama.

Tom emphasized this point time and again in his story conferences with movie executives and script writers in later years. He realized that in films some of the realities of the West had to be sacrificed in the interest of motion picture commercialism. But one thing he would not sacrifice was the true character and scope of the cowboy.

He resumed his real-life cowboy role for the fall roundup that year. He was eager to get back on the range again as a relief from his activities in Wild West shows.

I was glad for the breathing period too. Tom intimated that he was feeding on the idea of organizing another more elaborate Wild West show, and the idea most certainly did not appeal to me.

I was still too young then to know that Tom was going through a stage of confusion too. He had stepped abruptly from a life of adventure to a life—though a still highly unsettled one—of marital responsibility. It was an abrupt change for a man who had always been as free as the wide ranges he rode.

Tom came back from the roundup a month later and looked as though he'd swallowed an elixir.

"It was great to get into it again," he said, smiling. "But I was counting the days till I could get back to you."

I was happy, having counted the days myself, again and again. I urged him to tell me about the roundup, having never seen one.

"Well," said Tom, "Bill and the other ranchers insisted that I be the captain. It took me a couple of days to get all the duties assigned and the provisions laid out, and then we set out with about fifty men and a half-dozen wagons and five hundred horses."

The usual ratio of horses to men in a roundup was ten to one. A roundup meant sixteen hours in the saddle at a time, and it called for frequent changes to fresh horses.

"Each morning the camp was moved to a new spot," Tom explained, "and we spread out on both sides and drove the cattle into the new camping place. Then, in the afternoons, we separated the brands, and branded the mavericks with the brands of the cows they followed."

He went on to tell me that during the nights each wagon took its turn at guarding the collected animals. The whole roundup was a cooperative venture of the various ranchers of the region.

"The final stage, after the strays were brought in, was sorting the animals for market and getting them off for shipment," he told me. "We had good luck on this roundup—only a couple of minor stampedes."

A cattle stampede can be a dreadful thing. Once aroused by a storm or by almost any kind of unusual noise, a herd of cattle can sweep across a piece of range like an avalanching mountain, destroying everything—man, animal, and inanimate object alike—in its path. Few people outside the West realize how dangerous a cattle roundup really is. It is thousands upon thousands of animals against a few men trying to direct and control them. The odds are enormous. It takes only one incendiary moment to bring death. The roundup is only one more manifestation of the cowboy's skill, strength and endurance.

"Well, what next?" I said to Tom one morning after the roundup was over.

We didn't need to figure that out, for Tom's future had already been decided for him. The letter from the Selig Studio in Chicago arrived that very day.

Tom's first contract with Selig covered a period of one year. He wasn't particularly enthusiastic about going into films for such a long period of time, for he still wanted to buy a ranch in Arizona. It seemed to be his favorite state.

I once again reminded him that "we" had a ranch in Oklahoma. He just looked at me without speaking. I read his thoughts. He still wanted a ranch that he could develop himself—*our* ranch. And also he knew that our place in Oklahoma, although big, did not have the broad sweep of thousands of acres that he had in mind.

He signed the contract because he felt that the films, with a steady salary, would get us to this ranch objective much more quickly than Wild West shows would ever do.

He certainly was not expecting any spectacular film stardom, though he was to achieve the basis of his immense popularity in the eight years, from 1910 to 1918, that he reigned as Selig's most valuable property. The real glitter of his fame came when he moved on to bigger and better pictures with William Fox Studios in the postwar era. The decade after the armistice proved to be the biggest era and the point of maturity for the silent film.

Theater owners cried for more and more Western films. Though the American movie-going public was rapidly becoming a gigantic maw that demanded all types of variety to satisfy its palate, the saga of the development of the West was what it liked best.

"Westerns are the biggest money-makers," Will Dickey said. "The great romance of American life comes right out of what happened in the winning of the West."

American motion pictures were being shipped abroad, and audiences in foreign countries also loved these epics of a life that could be found only in our country.

Tom's pictures for Selig reaped an enormous financial harvest for the company and indeed prevented its bankruptcy during those harassing days when patent lawsuits and antitrust actions threatened the existence of all but the richest of the motion picture companies.

During this period Tom shared the throne of real Western stardom with William S. Hart, who worked for a rival company. The two were equally popular, both here and in Europe, for several years; but Tom's star was to shine much more brightly than William S. Hart's in the postwar era, and he was destined to have a much longer reign, one that lasted for almost thirty years, right up to the moment of his death.

Tom made twelve two-reelers for Selig in 1910. It was a good time for him to enter pictures, for the screen had at last really begun to move. To the end of the first decade of the century, the motion picture camera had served as a stationary eye rather than a moving one. Now it moved with the action. This development was very important in the type of films Tom made. The screen had literally come alive. Audiences wanted to see action, and the faster the better. They would no longer accept the static unrealities of the very early films, which were produced as a succession of short scenes played in front of a stationary camera.

Shortly after we arrived in Chicago, Tom and I were both assigned to appear in minor roles in a Selig film featuring Harry Pollard, Marguerite Fisher, and Mary Mannering. Selig was merely making use of our time while a new Western film was being written for Tom. The profits from *The Range Rider*, even though the picture had barely been released by that time, were already far exceeding expectations, and Selig was busy laying plans for a whole series of Tom Mix films.

In the meantime, we were "utilized" during the waiting period. I must admit that Tom looked a little stiff in the formal evening suit he was required to don, though I was thrilled with the elaborate evening gown I was to wear. The film was a drawing-room drama, the only film of that type Tom ever appeared in. It was notable not only for Tom's brief appearance in it as an English nobleman, but also because it introduced Wallace Reid to the screen. Wallace had a very minor role, but the film was his springboard to the perch he held eventually as one of the most popular lovers of the silent screen.

Between scenes we all pitched in to help get properties and scenery ready for the next take. In those early days film-making was a really cooperative venture. When they weren't acting before the cameras, actors were painting the canvas backdrops for the next scene. Directors and cameramen, when no shooting was going on, were busy with hammer and saw, building sets. Technicians served as actors and extras when required. The great day of specialization, when actors did nothing but act and directors did nothing but direct, was to come in later years when the star system was entrenched and when unionization thrust its wedge into the industry.

In those days, of course, there were no sound stages. Interior scenes were built on a huge platform with walls on four sides. The ceiling of these crude structures consisted of a series of strips of white canvas worked with pulleys, so that the sunlight could be regulated by letting in as much as needed.

There were no huge banks of lights, and as a rule only one camera. A husky assistant always went along with the cameraman to move around the clumsy contraption with its heavy tripod, or carry it up hill and down dale. When a scene called for moving from a long shot to a close-up, the camera had to be moved manually. There were no dollies or electrical booms to make these maneuvers easy.

By the time the drawing-room drama was completed, the script for Tom's next film was ready; so we went to Tennessee for the filming.

The second film was even more crammed with violent action than *The Range Rider* had been. The biggest scene in this picture involved Tom's leaping on horseback down thirty feet into a lake. This trick had never been done before in the movies, and it left movie-goers gasping throughout the breadth of the nation.

Tom emerged from the violence of this film with one broken tooth and two broken ribs. After brief hospitalization he was thoroughly mended again. I was already becoming used to having him sacrifice his personal safety to his career. The prospect of danger and broken bones never daunted him in his quest to give all of himself to the public that grew to adore him.

Colonel Zack Mulhall, in whose show Tom had appeared with Will Rogers at the St. Louis Fair in 1904, tracked us down

on location just as Tom finished the picture. Zack was putting
on a show at the Appalachian Exposition in Roseville, Tennessee, and he wanted Tom to star in it. Since we had three
free weeks before we had to report to Florida for Tom's next
picture, we accepted the offer.

We found a star's tent waiting for us in the show camp at
Roseville. Zack even provided an Oriental rug for his star performer. Tom was elated to get back into a show before a live
audience again, and he gave a performance of daring tricks
that brought howls of acclamation from the spectators, and
tears of appreciation from Zack.

One night Theodore Roosevelt was in the audience. There
was nothing reticent in Mr. Roosevelt's nature, and when
Tom made his grand entry on Old Blue, Mr. Roosevelt rose
from his seat and started shouting greetings to Tom. The two
men talked back and forth before a vastly amused audience.

After the show Mr. Roosevelt had dinner with us. At first I
could hardly get a word in anywhere while he and Tom
swapped reminiscences of the Spanish-American War.

"Yes, sir," Theodore Roosevelt said, "the Rough Riders
were the finest bunch of men I've ever had the pleasure of
working with."

A large proportion of the Rough Riders had been cowboys
and men of the plains such as Tom. Regardless of the worldly
circles Mr. Roosevelt moved in during his political career, he
still felt closest to the men who had led the "strenuous life."
He loved the West and had poured that love into a four-
volume history called *The Winning of the West*, the most
comprehensive coverage of Western development up to that
time. He gave us an autographed set of his volumes on the
West before he left town.

We prepared to leave for Florida then. So far 1910 had
been an important year for us, though at that moment we
weren't really aware just how important it was.

5

A Bare Little Place Called Hollywood

WE FOUND THE WHOLE COMPANY ASSEMBLED AND WAITing when we reached Dixieland Park in Jacksonville, Florida.

This time Tom was to step out of his role of cowboy to appear with Kathlyn Williams in a jungle film. Kathlyn was the first of the "serial queens." Her "Adventures of Kathryn" films for Selig were the prologue to the later "peril" series that Pearl White appeared in during the years of World War I.

Making the jungle film was a lot of fun for all of us. It was Tom's first experience with circus animals. The menagerie, which had been rented from an animal trainer by the name of Tom Persons, consisted of an elephant called Toddles, a camel named Elmer, a lion known as Charlie, and three nameless leopards. For the most part the animals seemed to be fairly docile, but Tom Persons had to be retained all during the shooting, for there is no such thing as a tamed wild beast. Before the picture was finished we had substantial proof of that.

Toddles was a huge pachyderm with evil-looking eyes. Kathlyn Williams, who had to ride on Toddles' head in several scenes of the picture, tried to prepare the path for friendship by throwing an armful of oranges to Toddles every morning. Toddles loved oranges, but he invariably picked them up in his trunk and threw them right back at her.

He was, we discovered, a one-man elephant, and the object of his devotion was Tom. He would trumpet gaily any time Tom was near. He had a habit of winding Old Blue's tail in his trunk and following along like a sheep dog when Tom went down the beach on his horse.

Toddles also had a habit of getting into trouble. One night Tom and I were awakened by an irate warehouseman.

"That blasted elephant's shooting beans all over the place!" he exclaimed.

Toddles had broken his chain, walked calmly out of camp, and had settled down amid some barrels of navy beans on the loading platform of a nearby warehouse.

Quite a crowd had collected by the time we got there. Toddles was trumpeting and spraying the air and the onlookers with showers of beans!

When Toddles saw Tom, he stopped spraying, hung his trunk, and actually looked sheepish. Tom led him right back to camp with a firm hold on one of his big, floppy ears.

Toddles liked to dip his trunk into the camp coffee pots and do his spraying act with coffee grounds.

The elephant's worst prank happened one night when he broke his chain and made a nocturnal foray on the leopards' cages. Somehow he managed to dump the cages open with his trunk and, before the racket thoroughly awakened the camp, the leopards had streaked off into the night.

Tom, the animal trainer, and two men from the production crew set off to track the leopards. They found them four miles from camp and captured them by throwing fishermen's nets over them—a scheme devised by Tom to trap the animals. The city of Jacksonville slept peacefully through it all.

And the very next day Tom saved Kathlyn Williams' life.

A leopard had been trained to pounce on a chicken for this particular scene of the film. Perhaps the scene would have gone off as planned had not a sudden gust of wind blown Kathlyn's long, loose, blond hair. The movement diverted the leopard's attention from the chicken, and he sprang at Kathlyn instead.

She landed on the ground, her eyes wide with horror. The leopard hovered over her, pausing for just a moment, as though he were waiting to see if she was going to fight back at him.

"Lie perfectly still, Kathlyn," Tom called over quietly. He pulled his gun.

One shot and the leopard was finished. Kathlyn rose, terribly shaken, but uninjured except for a few scratches. The cameraman ground right on through it all and the scene proved to be one of the highlights of the film.

Because of the complications with the animals, it took over a month to film that two-reel jungle thriller. We didn't mind; pay day was every Saturday.

The day of huge salaries for movie people was still a few years away. Just as they were to lead the way in the establishing of the star system, Mary Pickford and Charles Chaplin were also to be responsible for the system of big salaries for stars. In the end Tom's weekly stipend was as high as that of any other star. He made as much as $17,500 a week when he was at the crest of his career at William Fox Studios, and drew $20,000 a week as the star of the Sells-Floto Circus in the late twenties and early thirties.

But in his early days with Selig, Tom's salary was only a tiny fraction of those fabulous amounts. Each pay day he would hand over his salary to me to add to our growing ranch fund.

"You take care of the money, Olive," he said. "I don't know how."

It was quite true that Tom had difficulties in his handling of money at various points in his life. Before his death he had made and lost several fortunes. Money was certainly never a whip over him, yet he was to find himself at times, in later years, at the mercy of it. The periods of almost wanton extravagance and poor business investments that resulted in the loss of several of Tom's fortunes rose not only from his lack of control over money but also from the emotional tenseness that he found himself in during those periods. In the complex world of fame he was to lose touch on several occasions with the simple man of the plains that he started out to be. Those were bleak, unhappy years for him.

Before we were married I don't believe Tom thought about money at all. This disregard for riches was typical of most cowboys, who were content enough with food, shelter, clothing and sufficient tobacco money to squeak through on, as long as they could live the free range life they loved.

That Tom thought more about bringing law and order to the West than he did in getting money is revealed in a story his mother wrote me in one of her letters. It had to do with a

Tom's best and most representative photograph.

Tom Mix as a soldier (*front row, third from left*) at Fortress Monroe, Virginia, just after he returned from the Spanish-American War and just before he left to fight in the Philippine Insurrection.

Will Rogers, the beloved cowboy-humorist, who introduced Tom Mix to Olive Stokes.

Tom and Olive Mix shortly after their marriage.
The dog, Tag, Tom had rescued from coyotes.

Olive Mix roping and tieing a steer in Dewey,
Oklahoma.

Tom and some cowboy friends at Flemington,
Missouri, where the Selig Co. made its first picture
with him.

Tom Mix (*left*) and his mother (*center*) with a
friend, outside Tom's private circus car.

Tom and Ruth Mix when Ruth was six months old.

Tom Mix walking on Vine Street, in Hollywood, at the height of his fame as an actor.

Tom with Tony (*left*) and Old Blue (*right*).

Tony, who had been pining during Tom's serious illness due to an accident, visits his convalescent master on the lawn of Tom's Beverly Hills home.

Tom in his complete "outfit."

Tom by the fireplace of his home, which was one of the show places of Beverly Hills.

Tom Mix as star of his own circus.

Tom astride Tony in one of their movies.

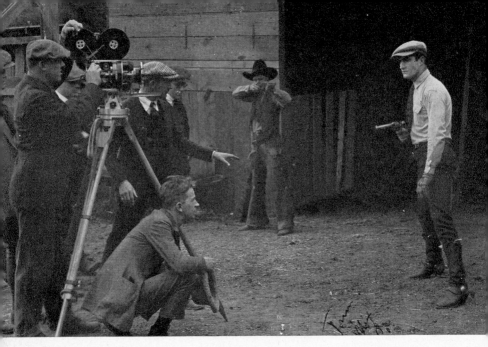

An early Tom Mix movie, made at the Fox Studio.
Sid Jordan holds a rifle ready to shoot a real bullet.

Shooting a scene on location for one of Tom's
early silent movies.

n thought nothing of risk-
life and limb to give the
ic a thrill when he was
making his movies.

this real bridge collapses
a real river, Tom and
y have another narrow
pe together while making
pictures.

Tony carries Tom—and a dummy—over a solid
iron gate for this scene in a 1924 movie.

Tom and Tony prepare to bring the wicked to
justice.

A scene from *The Broncho Twister*, a Fox picture of 1927.

Tom rescues another damsel in distress, this time in *Fourth Horseman*, a Tom Mix production for Universal in 1933. Fred Kohler and Marguerite Lindsay are the other actors.

The great stage at Mixville in the process of construction.

Photographing a scene on one of the permanent sets at Mixville.

Ruth Mix as co-star of her father's circus.

Tom's last picture, taken with his daughter Ruth just before his fatal accident.

The monument to Tom Mix near Florence, Arizona. The inscription reads: "In memory of Tom Mix, whose spirit left his body on this spot, and whose characterizations and portrayals in life served better to fix memories of the Old West in the minds of living men."

notorious outlaw combination, the Shontz brothers, who carried on their nefarious activities in eastern Oklahoma.

The brothers, two of the most vicious outlaws of the West, perpetrated almost every type of crime imaginable. They would, for example, shoot a man simply for the pleasure it gave them to see him die whereas most bandits—even the worst ones—killed other men only in self-defense or when it was necessary to do so in making an escape. The Shontz brothers were as elusive as eels. When Tom finally caught up with them they had carried on their fiendish schemes without punishment for several years.

Tom, serving at the time as an honorary deputy sheriff, finally tracked them to a Mexican woman's sod hut deep in the prairie, and waited patiently at the mesquite corral until one of the brothers emerged at daylight to feed the horses.

"Get your hands up!" Tom called out.

Shontz dug at his holster and whipped his gun up. His shot rang out simultaneously with Tom's. Shontz died instantly and Tom's leg buckled from the bullet he took in his knee.

The noise brought the younger Shontz brother out with his gun blazing. Tom was weaving on his injured leg, but his aim was still good enough to shoot the outlaw's gun out of his hand. Tom felled him with a shot in the leg, then hobbled up to him and lifted the man onto his horse. The younger brother was still alive and destined to stand trial for the multitude of crimes he had committed.

But Tom did not escape without further injury. As he started back toward town with the outlaw strapped to the saddle, the Mexican woman came out of the hut with a double-barreled shotgun. She blazed away at Tom and he took a heavy peppering, one so thorough that bits of shot were still being removed from his back years later in Hollywood.

Despite his riddled back, which burned like lava fire, and his crippled knee, Tom got safely back to town with the younger Shontz.

The reward money for the Shontz brothers was twenty-five hundred dollars, a large sum in those days and a fortune to Tom, whose monthly stipend ranged from twenty to sixty dollars, depending upon whether he happened to be a cowboy or a sheriff at the moment.

Twenty-five hundred dollars would have been a nice start on the ownership of the ranch he had always dreamed about. But without thought to his own interest, he turned over the entire reward to the bereaved mother of the Shontz brothers, a fine old lady whose life had been turned into horror from worry over her outlaw sons. In view of the fact that he had killed one of her sons, Tom felt in a way beholden to her.

When, in his capacity as a law officer, it was necessary for Tom to kill a man, he was always deeply affected by it. Basically he was a gentle man, with a deep respect for human life. He was not at any time trigger-happy, as some other marshals and many outlaws were.

His passion for justice transcended his horror of killing. The Shontz brothers had killed more than a score of men and had eluded law officers and posses alike for several years before Tom killed one of them and delivered the other to justice. In this case he killed, as in every other one when he was forced to do so, only to remove a menace from society.

Perhaps if Tom had served as a Western law officer a decade or so earlier than he did—in the cattle-trail days, when the West was in the throes of its greatest violence—Tom would have ended with a bullet in his heart, just as so many of the other famous marshals of the West did. Violence begot violence and the odds against survival were just as great for the law protectors as they were for the gunmen outlaws whom they fought.

Tom's death, when it came, was in a moment of sudden violence, but not from a bullet.

After we left Florida we hopped around to various states for the filming of the nine other moving pictures Tom made for Selig in 1910. I was constantly packing and unpacking, it seemed, but at least we always spent from two weeks to a month in each location. We would have moved much more frequently had we been involved in ranch shows that year.

The year 1910 came to an end and so did Tom's contract. Nobody said a word about renewing it.

"Well," I said to Tom, "what's next?"

It seemed as though I asked that question more frequently than any other during the period of my marriage to him.

"We'll go down and stay with your mother for a while," Tom said. "We'll figure out something to do."

Without asking, I knew what that meant. I had a strong feeling Tom was going to propose that we take a flyer on another ranch show.

I didn't want that at all. My intuition about Wild West shows was borne out with deadly accuracy in later years. Tom's involvement with ranch shows and, in later years, with his own circus, was responsible for the major financial disasters that came to him.

At home I said, "I just can't understand why Mr. Selig let you slip away without renewing your contract."

"Guess he doesn't think I'm good enough for films," Tom said with his customary modesty.

That was ridiculous for Tom's films, even during that first year, were immensely popular and had earned their cost of production many times over.

This oversight of Selig's in not immediately renewing Tom's contact was, we discovered later, a result of the complete disorganization that visited the Chicago studio in the late months of 1910. Everything came to a dead stop while the studio heads pondered what their next move would be.

For 1910 had been a year of even more than the usual flux in the motion picture industry. Selig had joined the other major producing companies in a patent-sharing agreement and a joint renting business intended to dominate the film distribution market. In this war for the survival of the fittest, many of the smaller independent producing outfits died of economic strangulation. But some of them escaped to southern California, where process servers were notable by their absence.

The agreement among the major companies proved to be unsatisfactory to Selig. And the Edison Co. was continuing its badgering with its constant suits of patent infringement; Edison argued that any kind of machine which recorded picture on film was a violation of his patents.

Early in 1911, Selig decided to leave the combine and move to California. The sparsely populated suburbs around Los Angeles were destined to be the headquarters of the independent producing companies.

Shortly after this decision was made we received a letter from W. N. Selig, the head of the company. He wanted Tom to come to Chicago at once to sign a new contract.

Tom hesitated. "I don't know whether I want to go back again," he said. He had been talking about starting a Wild West show again.

"Remember the ranch fund," I said cautiously. "It is going to need a lot more of those movie paychecks before we'll be able to get the kind of ranch you want, Tom."

That settled it. We went to Chicago and Tom signed the contract. Then we left with a company of players to make a picture near Canyon City, Colorado.

Our production camp was in the mountains above the timber line, a beautiful location of magnificent panoramic views. The air was tonic pure.

Tom loved this invigorating country and so did I. So did the rest of the cast, which included Tom Carrigan, Myrtle Steadman, and William Duncan. The cast and the production crew, most of whom were Eastern tenderfeet, were soon infected with the Western spirit.

In the early evening, after the day's work was done, we would all gather in the cold pure air to sit around the campfire and sing and talk. It was mostly talk, for the cast and the production crew kept urging Tom to tell his tales of the Old West. And Tom, though he was never a talkative man, became loquacious when telling about his greatest love, the West, and about his own personal hero, the cowboy image.

"Lots of stories of the Old West got blown up a thousand times before they finished making their rounds of the East," Tom would say. "Everybody was crazy to hear about what the outlaw did and what the Indian fighter did. And about the trouble the wagon trains had and about all the adventures that came with the gold rushes and the Indian wars and the Pony Express. The cowboy sort of got hidden away under all that, and it's too bad, because he was the most important man of all."

In 1911, when we sat around that campfire in Colorado, the cowboy's day of glory had been over for almost twenty years. It had begun with the opening of the cattle trails after the end of the Civil War and had ended in the early nineties when various pressures brought an end to the vast cattle movements through the Western states. But during his twenty-year span of reign as king of the West, the cowboy left a unique mark on Western history that has never been paralleled.

And of all the cowboy stars who have brought the cowboy's

story to the screen, Tom probably did more than any other to preserve the legend and to give it its proper scope and glory.

When Tom laughed it was no weak chuckle. It was loud enough to echo in the canyon one morning in Colorado when I stood before him, looking far from my usual self.

"Olive, I never would have known you!" Tom whooped.

I laughed too. "You're in for a *real* surprise," I said. "I'm going to play the part of your mother in the next scene."

The art of screen make-up was in its most rudimentary stage in those days. My face had been covered with cold cream and then heavily powdered to give it a dead white appearance. A few charcoal lines gave me wrinkles. A can of powder combed into my hair gave me the final bit of senescence needed for the scene. In those days, fortunately, audiences were inclined to overlook small defects as long as the semblance to life was at least partly retained.

So I played the role of Tom's mother in that film. Later I played the same role in several other films Tom made for Selig. Tom made a big joke of it and would often taunt me by introducing me to his friends as his mother. Tom was basically a serious-minded person, but he liked his fun too. He was a great one for playing inoffensive pranks on others, and he enjoyed having them played on him. In later years at certain points along the way he almost lost his capacity to find fun in life. Those were the black moments that came after Tom's way of life got too big to accommodate even his own personal bigness.

I remember one funny episode that occurred when Tom was at the height of his career in Hollywood. He had made a bet with a well-known actor of those times, Tom Kennedy, a man over six feet tall and weighing over two hundred pounds. Tom bet Kennedy that Jack Dempsey would beat Tunney; it was just prior to that famous battle between the heavyweights. Kennedy wagered two hundred dollars, plus a ride pickaback on the sturdy Mix shoulders. As now written in the history books, Dempsey lost. Tom's payment of his bet is also written in the memory of several thousand people who witnessed that famous ride.

Kennedy arrived at the appointed spot on Sunset Boulevard with his pocket full of bricks. These were removed by Tom Mix admirers, who also presented the winner of the bet with an unexpected blow in the conventional spot when he had mounted on Mix's shoulders. The board which hit Kennedy had been arranged to fire a blank cartridge. The wrong side of the instrument was presented to the winner's anatomy, however, with the result that the cartridge, instead of being blown into space, made a neat bull's-eye on the seat of the unlucky rider's trousers. After the fire had been extinguished, Tom added a suit of clothes to the things he owed the winner.

In 1911 the agonies that sometimes accompany fame were still a hazy blur in Tom's crystal ball. We all had a great deal of fun making the Colorado picture. Tom was popular with the rest of the cast and with the production crew, as he always was with everyone he worked with. He would treat a prop boy as though he were his closest friend. His warm regard for people reached out and permeated everyone he came in contact with. Even in his great starring days he behaved toward everyone he knew and met with great respect and humility. Some of the big stars of the screen were notorious for their tumultuous temperament and their disregard for the dignity of others, but never for a moment did Tom fit into that category. His regard for other people was one of his most lovable traits.

He was always thinking of what he could do to help others. Even when we were isolated in the mountains of Colorado, he thought of a plan to bring some cheer into some very gray lives.

The Colorado penitentiary was located in Canyon City. Tom whipped up a show among the members of the film cast and we spent an hour every Sunday at the prison entertaining the prisoners. Tom did his lasso tricks and Myrtle Steadman, who had a lovely voice, sang many songs for the hundreds of convicts. The response of the imprisoned men was almost rapturous.

This was merely a forerunner of the many benefit performances Tom gave during his long career. Even when he was a great star and pressed for time to fulfill his business commitments, he never hesitated to take time out to do a charity show. If the cause was worthy, if people needed help, he was always on hand to help.

When it came to attending clubs and banquets to act as guest speaker, however, Tom always tried to find a way to renege. In later years when our daughter Ruth became his constant companion, he would send her to fulfill these engagements in lieu of himself. Unlike her father, Ruth enjoyed these meetings and generally managed to overcome the disappointment of Tom's non-appearance.

Mr. Selig came to Colorado just as we finished the film.

"I'm on my way to the coast," he informed us. "The new studio is about finished and we'll be moving all our production out there within the next year or so."

"Where is the California studio located?" Tom asked.

"In some foothills near Los Angeles," Mr. Selig replied. "It's just a bare little place, and you've probably never heard of it. It's called Hollywood."

6

Ruth – and Tony

It was to be a while, however, before we were to see Hollywood.

With the Colorado picture wrapped up, there was no film planned for Tom for the immediate future. This would be a good time for a vacation, I thought. But I was wrong.

A letter came from Guy Weadick, a New York impresario.

"He's planned to put a show on in Calgary, Alberta," Tom said. "He says he'd like to talk to me about being in it."

I submitted to the idea with a repressed sigh. My experience with our own show in Washington had soured me on them forever.

Later I came to understand why Tom preferred appearing in ranch shows and circuses to appearing in films. Nothing evoked more response from him than having a living, breathing audience to play to. He would reach out and gather the audience in to himself, and the spectators realized how much he loved people. More than once I heard persons in the audience declare that Tom seemed to be playing to them alone, that he seemed to single them out specifically to give them the greatest performance of his career. He had the almost unique quality of being able to make everyone feel important. And to Tom everyone *was* important.

He didn't forget the importance of other people when he was in his starring years, either. He was probably more universally adored by children than any other star, before or since. They flocked to see his movies and great mobs of them hung about stage doors when he made his personal appearance tours in the later years. They hung on his every gesture and word, and he never failed to respond to their idolization. At the height of his career he was emulated by millions of children all over the world; there were hundreds of "little Tom Mixes" in even the smallest towns, most of them cleaning out a nest of imaginary outlaws in their backyards in typical Tom Mix fashion. The popular dream of the day was to grow up to be like Tom Mix.

His influence on children was indeed immeasurable; and his was an absolutely positive influence. Probably Tom's greatest contribution in his long career was the result of his steadfast purpose that his films should teach youth to be truthful and strong and fearless—and clean-living.

I was thrilled with New York City, though our stay there was brief. After the final arrangements for the show were made, Tom, Guy Weadick and I left for Calgary. While the show was being rehearsed there, I made several visits to the doctor.

When I told him, Tom responded like a typical man. At first he acted a little dizzy. Then he looked flushed. Then he burst into the most expansive smile of all time.

"A baby," he said with wonder in his voice. "A baby. A baby."

As though there had never been a baby born before!

I laughed, but Tom was already pacing the floor, smiling and making plans at a mile a minute.

"I've got to get there fast now," he said, smacking his fist against his palm with determination. "We've got to give our daughter everything in the world."

I never was able to figure out how he knew it would be a daughter.

He was so solicitous of me in my pregnancy that I could scarcely move without bringing a frown of worry to his face. I kept laughing and reminding him that pioneer women had had it much harder than I was going to have it; but Tom kept on treating me as though he were afraid I would break into halves if he even breathed in my direction.

The show in Calgary was very successful and made an enormous profit, which was true of most of the shows that he starred in for other people. It was only in the shows he backed with his own money that he had his bad luck.

But there was one very frightening episode that occurred while Tom was acting in the Weadick show, at Dominion Park in Montreal.

It was during a Sunday night performance. The moment came for the bulldogging of a steer. Tom came out into the arena as usual with an air of complete self-confidence. But as he leaped onto the steer and bore it to the ground the animal made a quick turn and the tip of a horn caught Tom at the base of the jaw, knocking him out cold. His jaw bleeding badly, he was carried from the arena to his dressing room.

He came to in a few moments and, immediately after opening his eyes, he said "Is it time for the bronc-busting?"

Johnny Mullens, one of the cowboys who was working with the show at the time and a top performer as well as an old friend of Tom's, tried to persuade Tom not to enter the bronc-riding event.

Needless to say, Tom went out and entered the bucking horse period of the program. It was an unlucky night for him. He had been jarred up by the steer more seriously than he calculated and the horse he was on, a ferocious animal with plenty of tricks, threw him.

Once again he was carried out of the arena. This time I called a doctor. Tom's face was badly cut and bleeding. The doctor came and stated that he would call an ambulance and go with Tom to the hospital.

Tom refused to go. I sensed that maybe he did not want me to go with him in an ambulance, so I whispered to Johnny Mullens to tell Tom that he would go along with him.

Finally Tom agreed.

Later that night I learned the rest of the story.

Tom would not let the doctor ride in the ambulance with him and Johnny Mullens. So the driver let the doctor ride beside him on the seat of the ambulance. It was a horse-drawn vehicle and the streets were cobblestone and tortuous to an injured person riding in a vehicle.

It was two or three miles to the hospital from the park. The driver of the ambulance was going as fast as the horses could trot and there was much rattling and squeaking. Tom was lying on the cot. Johnny said he raised himself up and said: "Listen, Johnny, I'm not going any further. I'll get out and you ride on. Then you get out and let them go on. They won't know we're gone."

Tom climbed out of the back door of the ambulance. Johnny rode on a few blocks and then decided that it was not such a good idea. He banged on the front of the ambulance and the driver pulled to a halt.

When the doctor learned that Tom had jumped from the

ambulance, he was scared, for he knew it would look pretty bad for him to show up at the hospital without his patient.

Under the doctor's instruction the ambulance was turned around and retraced its journey for several blocks until they saw Tom standing under an arc lamp, waiting for Johnny as planned.

They got him back into the ambulance. When they got to the hospital a little French nurse, who did not look to be over sixteen years old, was called in to help out. Tom stared at her and said in a very deep voice, "This is a nice time of night for a girl like you to be running around!" He flustered the girl so much she dropped everything she touched.

The doctor tried to get Tom to stay overnight at the hospital but Tom refused. "Doc," he said, "I'm not going to stay here when you got ghosts running around and fellows dying every few minutes."

Tom and Johnny left the hospital. The doctor had taped Tom's face until only his eyes were visible. They went to a corner to wait for a streetcar. Tom sauntered over to a plate glass window and saw an image of himself.

"I'm a devil of a looking sight!" he exclaimed. He ripped off the bandages and threw them into the gutter.

After the Calgary show was over we did two films for Selig, and then Tom joined Vernon Seavers' Young Buffalo Show in Peoria, Illinois. This was another successful affair, and when it was finished we went to Dominion Park again to do yet another show.

I was far along in my pregnancy then, and the first thing Tom did in Montreal was to line up a whole battery of doctors for me. As the time for the birth came closer and closer, I grew happier and happier, feeling certain that Tom would get the Wild West show sickness out of his system when our baby was born. Our itinerant life would have to end. I had become more and more dissatisfied with that mode of existence, and we had more than one disagreement about it.

In Montreal Tom spent most of his time talking to me and to everyone else about the baby we were going to have. There were a number of Indians in the show and it wasn't long before we were honored with many papoose garments which the squaws generously made for us. We made good use of them later. Ruth learned to walk in the moccasins a squaw made while we were in Montreal.

A few weeks before the baby was due to arrive I began to feel panicky. I had felt the pangs of homesickness many times in my peregrinations with Tom, but never to such an intense degree.

"Tom," I said, "I want the baby to be born at home."

He was bitterly disappointed, but he catered lovingly to my whim to go home for the big event. It was just about the hardest thing Tom ever had to do in his life.

At the train he said, "I'll be there just as soon as I can, Olive." And he was almost crying!

He had his commitment to finish in Montreal before he could come home, but he fully expected to arrive there before the baby was born.

As it happened Ruth Mix was born on July 13, 1912, about a week before she was expected. There was an explosion of celebration at the ranch because the "new princess" had been born.

Tom arrived from Canada three days after Ruth's entry into the world. He burst into the bedroom and just stared and stared at her for minutes and minutes. Then he grinned at me and said, "Looks like we've got the most wonderful cowgirl in the world, Olive."

Tom never changed his mind about his daughter. She was

the closest person to him in his life from the moment she was born. And she was to be the last person in the world to talk to him before he died.

In the second decade of the century "going to the movies" became an established pattern in American life, and with this pattern came the longer picture. Two-reelers gave way to four- and five-reelers, and the old nickelodeon and tent shows gave way to big motion picture theaters designed especially to appeal to the steadily growing movie audience.

The star system came in, to stay, in the early days of World War I. The screen comedy got its real foothold in the war years, too, but the Western film continued to maintain its popularity—a popularity that has never really waned greatly over the years.

The struggle for the West offered a treasury of material for the movies to draw upon. The whole enormous story of the land west of the Mississippi made an incredibly wide base for drama. Audiences clamored for adventure, and Tom Mix, William S. Hart and Douglas Fairbanks gave the movie-goers every type of adventure imaginable.

Tom, who had entered films really as a stopgap measure, was soon enthusiastic about his movie career. "In the movies we can reach millions with our story," he said. "With ranch shows we can only reach thousands."

Tom's true knowledge of the adventures he was reliving on the screen proved of invaluable aid to the script writers who fashioned his pictures. He looked askance at any deviation from authenticity and was instrumental in keeping fantasy out of his films.

He realized the public demanded violence in films of the West. There wasn't much room for humor in the early Westerns, and there wasn't much room for the routine life that was as much a part of Western life as violence. This disturbed

Tom. "The public will get the impression that Westerners spent twenty-four hours a day shooting it out with one another," he said.

But that was the impression the movie-goer wanted to have and, consequently, it was the reason the early Westerns were based on tragedy rather than humor. In Tom's later pictures he managed to incorporate both facets of Western life in a nicely blended recipe.

There was a period, just after Ruth was born, when Tom thought of giving up his motion picture career.

"We have a baby now," he said. "A child has to have solid ground to grow up on. We've got to get settled."

"That's fine with me," I returned. There was nothing I wanted more in the world.

He spent three restless months at home trying to decide what to do. Then, just about the time his current contract with Selig was due to expire, a letter came from the Chicago studio asking Tom to report to Chicago and sign a new contract.

"I'm going to write and tell them I'm not interested," Tom said.

I hesitated for a long time. "You *are* interested," I eventually told him firmly. "And we are going to Chicago."

This meant final acknowledgment to myself that there was never going to be a real "settling down" in our lives. This feeling of mine was substantiated in later years. His restlessness had been born of his roaming days on the range. It was a seed that was planted deep in him, and it was compounded of his past life and the boundless energy he carried with him throughout his career. The later emotionalism that resulted from Tom's losing contact, at times, with the man he really was, further accentuated the seed of restlessness he always carried in him. It came to be at certain points in his life an escape hatch with him.

So, with this realization firmly entrenched in my mind, I went to Chicago with Tom. The new contract was signed and he made a picture at the Chicago studio. Ruth and I held forth in a hotel room. I had become very much accustomed to that type of living—not that I liked it, but I was certain that as Tom's wife I would be doing a good bit more of it as time went on.

I was in for a surprise when we arrived in Prescott, Arizona, for Tom's next picture. The company provided a furnished house for us. We had been married four years and this was our first real home.

I was delighted to be able, at last, to show my ability as a homemaker, and dreaded the finishing of that film which would mean our packing up and moving on!

Tom and Ruth had a field day. He would rush home from the day's shooting and make straight for her crib. He did lasso tricks while she gurgled up happily at him.

"I think she's grown an inch today," he announced.

"Don't be silly," I laughed.

He was perpetually making plans for her. "We'll have to get a horse for her," he said.

"Don't you think you'd better wait for a few years?"

"She's going to love the ranch when we get it," he said with a faraway look in his eyes.

"You're going to turn our daughter into a cowgirl?" I demanded. I remembered the struggles my mother had gone through with me as a child. "Not if I can help it! She can learn how to handle a horse but she's also going to know how to handle a teacup."

Ruth grew up with a high facility for doing both. She was a champion rider, an expert markswoman, and an accomplished roper. And she could handle her teacup as daintily as anyone else. She also grew up to be the fortress her father sought refuge behind in his blackest moments.

The news came through after we finished the film in Arizona that all of Selig's production of Western films was henceforth to be concentrated in Hollywood.

I was delighted to get to Hollywood. It might be a chance for us to settle down for a fairly long period of time.

In 1913 Los Angeles had grown from a tiny Spanish pueblo to a bustling city of almost four hundred thousand population, lying in a flat plain that spreads from the mountains and their foothills to the sea. Though the city was already sprawling toward its eventual metropolitan greatness, the suburbs were barely in their early-blossom stage. Hollywood, situated in the foothills of the Santa Monica Mountains, with the Cahuenga Valley lying below, was largely farm land and orange groves when the first motion picture studio was established there in 1911. Its big growth was not to come until after 1920, when it became acknowledged as the motion picture capital of the world.

Contrary to common conception, the motion picture companies did not settle in California because of its delightful climate but rather to avoid the litigation that was continually hovering on their backs when they were situated in the East. But the movie industry couldn't have made a happier choice than California for its new home. The varied topography offered exotic settings right in the studios' backyards—mountain, sea, and desert were close at hand. The weather was dependable, and outdoor shooting could be carried on between May and November with almost certain assurance there would be no interruption from rain. The weather had been a serious deterrent to movie production in the East until a satisfactory method of indoor set lighting was developed.

From 1913 onward Hollywood was the base of Tom's movie operations. It was also as near to being his home as any place could be to a man of his unsettled nature. Yet even though he began in Hollywood when just a few bungalows and small studios studded its beautiful hills and stayed on to see it become a place of palatial residences and enormous studios in the twenties, Tom's relationship with Hollywood was always a tenuous one. His body was in Hollywood and the present, but his mind and heart were in the plains and the past. The conflict between the "Old Tom" and the "New Tom" caused much of the dissatisfaction that came to him in later years.

Tom, Ruth and I settled in a bungalow that first year. And that year, too, Selig acknowledged openly that Tom was the studio's greatest asset. Tom was given his own studio in Glendale and the Selig-Tom Mix Company was formed.

It was about this time that Tom acquired Tony, the horse that was to become identified with him for many years.

Although there have been various stories as to the way Tom acquired Tony, the truth is that an actor friend of Tom's by the name of Pat Crisman one day spied a chicken wagon driving down one of the streets of Edendale. Alongside the horse drawing the vehicle was a black colt. The owner of the chicken wagon wanted to sell it. Pat Crisman purchased the colt, reared and trained him, and later sold him to Tom, who took an immediate liking to the black two-year-old when he happened to see him. Tom paid six hundred dollars for Tony.

Tony was to become the most famous show horse in the world for many, many years. He appeared with Tom in all the films he made from 1914 to 1932, replacing Old Blue who, in his old age, was retired to royal pasturage after years of devoted service to his master. Old Blue was buried in Mixville, the focal point of Tom's picture production while under the William Fox banner. Over the grave of Old Blue Tom had erected a big 4x4 wooden pillar with a projecting beam, so that he would be able to hang a wreath of flowers over the resting place of his faithful friend whenever he was in the vicinity.

During the thirty-four years that Tony lived no person except Tom ever sat on his back. No person other than Tom ever taught him a trick.

The two, Tom and Tony, were almost as inseparable in real life as they were on the screen. Literally millions of still photographs captioned TOM MIX AND TONY appeared all over the world during their long years of fame together. While at the height of his fame Tom received thousands of fan letters a week. So did Tony.

Tony didn't understand Tom's words, but he did understand over him was almost uncanny. When they were about to do a difficult scene, Tom would pat Tony on his nose and say, "Now, look, Tony, here's the way we're going to do this. . . ."

And that was the way they would do it.

Someone once commented that Tony must certainly have understood what Tom said to him. That was wrong, of course. Tony didn't understand Tom's words, but he did understand Tom's love, and that was enough.

Tony was a beautiful horse, with the slender strong lines and glossy sorrel coat of a thoroughbred. He had "white sox" on his hind legs and a white line down his head. He did not have a gourmet's palate: even during the years when he was the most famous animal in the world and traveled in his own private railroad car, the delicacies in his life were apples, carrots, and bananas, and he favored them in that order. Other than these horse delicacies, he subsisted contentedly on plain horse fare. He did not taste sugar even once in his entire life.

Tony was constantly tuned for action. He came to know what was expected of him and he, like Tom, never failed to come through as expected, regardless of any danger involved. I always felt that Tony *knew* he was a star, that he would have bowed his head in shame rather than do anything unworthy of himself or Tom.

Tony loved me too. I will never forget whenever I came up

to him how he would run his lip up and down my arm in a gesture of affection.

Of course, in Tom's films of the late twenties it was necessary to have a double for Tony in some of the very difficult scenes. A horse named Buster, who closely resembled Tony in line and color, doubled for him in some of the most dangerous tricks. The make-up people would paint a stripe on Buster's face and whiten his feet so that he looked almost exactly like Tony.

Tony was definitely jealous of Buster, and would snort with fury when Tom climbed on Buster's back. But later, as Tony grew older, I actually believe he understood that Tom was trying to spare him in his old age.

One terrifying incident involving Tom and Tony occurred when a picture was being shot at Santa Cruz, California. The script called for Tom to ride Tony along a narrow trail flanked by towering mountains, in order to escape the outlaws. The villains, meanwhile, knowing he would come this way, had planted dynamite in the trail. The instant he passed the dynamite, the script called for it to be blown up.

The director pleaded with Tom not to risk himself and Tony on such a shot, but Tom would have none of that.

Atop one of the mountains, well out of camera range, the dynamiter stood with hands poised over the detonator.

Tom on Tony's back waved at the dynamiter, a signal for him to get ready.

When the director yelled, "Roll 'em," Tom galloped for the trail entrance between the mountain sides. He came into the trail while the dynamiter took his reading. But the reading was without the aid of instruments; sighting in a simple fashion, he closed one eye and squinted at the target. He was an old duck hunter and he knew enough to lead anything he was shooting at.

Now the "bird" was below, but he needed leading just the same. The dynamiter led him on—and on—and on—NOW!

The earth rose beneath Tom and Tony, carrying them up and over the side of the mountain which was coming down at them because of concussion. Earth and stone smothered horse and rider, for the dynamiter, while squinting into the sun above them, had let the detonator go at the exact instant Tom and Tony were over the hidden explosive.

Tony lay perfectly still, careful not to move until his master was safe. There was a gaping hole in the horse's side, but he waited for his master to be moved first. He only whinnied softly, although undoubtedly suffering great pain.

They wanted to take Tom in an ambulance, but he wouldn't leave until Tony had been administered to by a veterinarian.

Years ago a friend of mine, Sara Hamilton, wrote a little story about Tony. I am transcribing it from the torn and yellow pages that I have treasured throughout the years. It is called, *Tony Goes to Green Pastures*:

I knew the moment I saw my master walk across the meadow that he had something unpleasant to tell me. I stood under the eucalyptus tree and watched him come, his shoulders squared for some ordeal ahead, his steps lagging. He walked up and looked at me for a long second. He didn't lay his hand on me, for Tom Mix knows how I dislike to be patted or fondled. He just stood there.

"Tony," he said at last, "you and I have been buddies for a long time. We've been through hell and heaven together. But, Tony, the time has come when we've each got to go our own way. You understand, boy?"

He pointed at my weak leg. Yes, I understood. For a long time I had suffered with that leg but had tried to ignore it. I'd had a lot of aches in my life and couldn't believe that this one, too, wouldn't pass away. Then, during the making of our last picture, just as I leaped across a stream with Tom on my back, it had caught me—a sharp, stabbing pain. We both went down. I knew it would never be better.

"You're going to green pastures, Tony," he said. "You've earned a long rest. You know, don't you, old fellow, that often you've been just about the only friend I've had . . . the one thing in the world I could come to. Well, I'll not forget you now."

He laid his hand for just a moment on my head. Then he was gone.

I watched him out of sight, over the pasture gate. I was glad he had told me, man to man, with no sobbing heroics. He knew I wouldn't have liked that.

Yet, as I watched him go, my mind went back to the time he first spoke to me. That was after my first master had delivered me over to him. "Well, boy," he said, "you and I are going to be good friends from now on, aren't we?"

In the mornings he would ride me out to a place where a group of men waited with little boxes on legs and some bright lights. Tom would tell me very quickly just what I was to do, and somehow— don't ask me how—I knew exactly what he meant and why. We were doing those things so the little box on legs could make a picture of us. I was an actor!

I got to be a better actor, too, never hesitating to do anything Tom asked me. "Walk down to that tree, Tony, then stop and look back," he'd say, showing me just how he wanted it done. And I'd do it. Why, we thought nothing of leaping into burning buildings, dashing down dangerous chasms, or jumping off a pier into the ocean.

Tom would never try to force me when I refused to take a leap or jump. He'd hunt around until he discovered the loosened boulder or cracked earth that would have meant our death had we gone on. How I knew these things before people did is something I've often wondered about but could never reason out.

I learned how to look my best before a camera and when to stop acting. "Will you look at that horse?" a visitor on location once remarked in my hearing. "How he struts and acts before the camera, and the minute he's out of camera range he's right back to eating grass as nonchalantly as you please."

Huh, I thought to myself, why not? I'm not one of those actors that can't stop acting, even when there's no camera around!

But as soon as the sun reached a certain spot in the sky, I knew enough work had been done that day even if the men didn't. Just plain horse sense, I guess.

Anyway, at five I quit. And they knew it was no use to argue with me.

So they would lead me into my truck and take me back to my stable. How I loved to go fast in my truck! I'd paw loudly with my foot to go faster and often my driver would yell back at me, "For heaven's sake, Tony, I can't go any faster here or the cops will get us."

I had a weakness for fancy saddles and bright plaid blankets, and Tom knew it and understood. He liked bright, gay things himself. So once, when a strange groom placed a drab old blanket on my back, I was hopping mad. Do you think I'd budge? No sir. The groom couldn't understand it until finally someone who knew me spotted that blanket and replaced it with a nice plaid one, and then I went.

Tom decided to go to Europe. They slung me up in a hoist onto the ship and it was work, as I weighed ten hundred and fifty pounds and stood fourteen hands high. I was exercised around the deck of the ship every morning and really enjoyed it.

In England I was at a very fashionable stable, and never shall I forget the horse in the stall next to me. He was English, of course, and if ever I saw style and class, he had it. And was he snooty! He looked me up and down several times and gave one big sniff. But when he saw me making my own bed that night—I always arranged the hay with my foot to suit myself—I thought he would break out in spavins. But I didn't care. Tom was probably dunking his cake in his coffee at one of those big mansions I'd seen and not giving a picayune.

The next morning a young fellow was ushered into my stall. He reached out a hand to pat me and suddenly withdrew it. He sensed I wouldn't like it and that made a big hit with me. Here was a man who understood horses. When he left he placed his hand very gently on my head as if he were just shaking hands.

"Who was that?" I asked Mr. Highhat in the next stall.

"That," he answered, and I noticed a new note of respect in his voice, "is His Royal Highness, the Prince of Wales."

We traveled all over Europe with lords and dukes and ladies all eager to meet us. Just plain Tom Mix and I. It seemed strange.

Home again, we made personal appearances in twenty-five big cities. Children were sometimes disappointed when they saw me, for on the screen they imagined me black instead of sorrel. But they'd soon recognize me by my white feet and white face.

By the time we got back to Hollywood, Tom was a very rich man. He began building his big new mansion in a place called Beverly Hills. I was happy about the place, but inside me was a dreadful fear. Tom might not need me or want me any more with a grand new house and new friends. But I never let on. One day he came out to the ranch and said, "Hi, Tony, how's the boy?" I nodded. "Come on, I want to show you something," he said.

Soon we were passing beautiful homes on lovely, quiet streets and I knew we were in Beverly Hills. Suddenly, there it was—his grand new house. I knew it by the initials, T.M. on the gate. Tom was always one for putting initials on everything. I glimpsed a swimming pool and a tennis court.

"Know what this is, Tony?" Tom asked. "Step up here and give a look." It was a beautiful building right near the gate and was as grand, almost, as the house. I looked in. "You're home, old boy," Tom said.

The time came when we went into the circus. You should have seen me in that parade. Did I show them something? "Well," one of those fancy riding horses once sneered, "you'd think he was a trained horse or something the way he struts." And did I put that madam in her place. I told her about the blazing buildings, the yawning chasms, the daily chances with death that Tom and I took together. Trained horse, indeed!

"Besides," I said, "I want you to know I'm a movie star, known by thousands. And who are you?"

And that knocked the pink ribbon off her tail.

Then we came back to movie acting. We've made our best pictures, I believe, since our return from the circus. Tom was sick and nearly died, but outside of that we've been happier than we've been for a long time. Until my accident, and the realization that I couldn't go on much longer.

Now it's over, Tom tells me. For me, at least. All the thrills, the travel, and the excitement are done. No more crowds. No more movies.

Somehow I can't be sorry. I guess I'm tired. I've reached the ripe old age of twenty-three years, most of them spent with Tom. We've seen more and been more places than most people.

I am alone again—but happy—in green pastures. . . .

Tony was happy in his green pastures for a long time. He survived his master by four years, then was chloroformed in 1944 at the age of thirty-four, when he had become too old and sick to enjoy any longer the richness of his green pastures. I will never forget how Ruth cried when they called long distance to her home in Texas to ask her permission to put Tony to sleep.

In those early days in Hollywood Tom was given free rein in the production of his movies. With the release of each new film his star burned brighter, and it became obvious that he was secure in his new career. He began bringing his range friends to California to work in his films with him; among them Sid Jordan.

Tom's friendship with Sid dated back to the days when they had worked together on the enormous 101 Ranch near Bliss, Oklahoma. Together with the Miller brothers, who owned the ranch, they helped to organize the famous 101 Ranch Wild West Show, a stupendous Western theatrical effort which enjoyed fabulous success when it opened in Chicago in 1907. Tom was the foreman of the cowboys in this show, and it was largely due to his ability for organization that the show was such a hit.

It was in Chicago, in 1907, that Elinor Glyn, the famous English novelist, first met Tom and predicted that he would one day assume a role of real importance in the entertainment world. Miss Glyn, who later turned from novels to writing movie scenarios and who created the famous "It" personality for Clara Bow in the twenties, once commented that Tom was the most perfect specimen of manhood she had ever met. It was an opinion shared by many, many other persons too.

Tom's close friendship with Sid Jordan had deep roots in the old range days. The loneliness of range life made for hard, endurable, silent friendships based on intense loyalty. Tom's relationship with Sid had a foundation of the hardest granite, and it endured unwaveringly up to the moment of Tom's death.

Sid was a frequent visitor at our home. I was busy rearing Ruth and I could no longer go to the studio to watch the shooting of Tom's pictures, but by pressing Sid for information I could usually find out what harrowing scene Tom had performed before the cameras that day.

Sid would try to joke about it.

"Oh," he said once, "you didn't do much today, did you, Tom? All you did was roll over a cliff in a stage coach."

"That's about all," Tom grinned.

Tom actually had gone over a cliff in a stage coach that day. It was the final scene shot in that picture. Tom had saved it until the last because it was the most dangerous scene of the picture and the chances were heavy that he would land in the hospital with a concussion and his usual quota of broken bones. While he was in the hospital the writers could be working on the next script.

Fortunately he emerged from the scene with a number of cuts and bruises, but nothing worse. Any other man would probably have been killed doing it, or at least severely injured.

It wasn't long after that—about a month in fact—when I got a call that Tom was in the hospital. Arriving there, I found that this time Tom was seriously hurt. The doctors informed me that the outlook was not too good.

I did not learn the entire story until I returned home. Little Ruth had heard of her father's illness and was hysterical. Sid Jordan was there with her and after assuring Ruth that her daddy would be all right, we managed to get her off to bed.

"Now tell me all about it, Sid," I demanded.

Sid was not even as talkative as Tom, but I finally dragged out of him that they had been shooting a picture in the Los Angeles Stadium. Tom had conceived a scene in which two chuck wagons, each drawn by six-horse teams, were in a wild race. Tom was on Tony as an outrider, galloping neck and neck with the lead horses of the team nearest the rail. Suddenly a doubletree came loose. The lead horse fell, spilling Tony and Tom and pinning both of them against the rail while, in some macabre fashion, the four remaining horses, dragging the wagon as they dropped, caught the outside vehicle.

The dozen horses, the two wagons and the equipment they carried, all had to be removed before first aid could be rendered the unconscious Tom. Miraculously Tony was unhurt.

This time it was three weeks before Tom was back home and able to continue his work. He spent a lot of time sitting out in the sun thinking up new stunts for new pictures.

A combination of qualities saved Tom from sudden death in his danger-fraught movie stunts. The most important was his enormous courage. His was silent courage, not talked about, always expressed in his complete willingness to face terrible hazards without fear and without comment. His dauntlessness was as much a part of his nature as was the truth on which he based his mode of living. He carried his great courage with him throughout his entire life.

His fearlessness was only the instigating charge in Tom's daily performance of hazardous feats. His suppleness and physical strength, and his ability to relax his body in even the most harrowing moments helped him to complete successfully the dangerous tricks his courage allowed him to begin. His brain response was electric, and decisions made in a fraction of a second saved his life on more than one occasion.

Still, even though aware that if anyone could, Tom would emerge still breathing from his dangerous movie stunts, I lived each day in suspense, constantly dreading the call that would inform me of Tom's latest hospitalization, or of something worse. It was like sending the person closest to you in life off to a new war every day of the year, and not knowing whether he would come back from the battleground that night or not.

Tom knew the tension I suffered. It worried him. It also worried him that his life had become so complicated, because with each new picture his obligation to his growing public became a shade more important. And with fame comes complications.

More than once he wanted to turn back to look for the life he had been forced to leave behind him.

He was an established star when one day he said to me: "Where's everything gone wrong, Olive? This life we lead isn't right for us. What happened to our dream? Where's that ranch I wanted more than anything in the world?"

I had to swallow pretty hard before I could force myself to answer him. It was difficult not to be selfish at that moment. But the whole world was pressing against me, rubbing against my personal dream; for Tom belonged to the world by then, not just to Ruth and me. He was now too big a man to be confined to a ranch.

"You're an important man now," I told him. "Your obligation is to the people you are making happy . . . those children

all over the world. . . . I guess we'll just have to wait for
our personal dreams to come true. But the time will come,
Tom . . . the time when newer and younger men will take
your place. Then surely we can live the life we've always
wanted so much."

Tom paced restlessly around the room. He could never just
sit still and talk. His entire life was one of almost unceasing
movement.

Finally he turned to me. "We've got enough money to buy
one of the biggest ranches in the country. But I guess you're
right, Olive. I've started something that's bigger than I am."

And so Tom went on to make over three hundred pictures.
He was swept into the vortex entirely too deeply ever to be
able to swim out of it. He simply was not destined to live the
quiet life on the open range that he had always wanted as a
goal in life. He accepted the fact that his obligation to the
public ran in far deeper waters than his personal desires; and
at this point he put his personal dreams aside for good.

I remember sitting once in the rear of a sunlit auditorium in
Los Angeles listening to Tom address a graduating high school
class. This was something, incidentally, that he did throughout his entire career. No matter how busy he was with his
professional work, he never shunned his obligation to talk to
youth whenever he was asked.

That day Tom told his youthful audience, "You're bound
to come to a lot of unmarked roads in your lives. It's tough
to know which one to take sometimes. But if you build your
lives on clean thoughts and on clean living, the chances are
you'll be taking the right roads *all* the time."

I looked around the raptly attentive audience of youthful
worshipers, every eye focused unblinkingly on the tall, dark
hero who stood before them giving them his message of faith
and strength.

"You students wouldn't be sitting here now—and I wouldn't

be standing here talking to you—if our forebears hadn't had the strength and the drive and the love to fight for a good kind of country, and a good kind of life for all of us. We owe it to them as well as to ourselves to show that we're proud of the country they made for us and proud of the good lives they've made possible for us. If you live right—as your forebears did—the world will be right for you and you'll be doing something positive for the world too."

Tom paused and looked around the audience; and I'm sure that each student felt he was being singled out personally.

"Always remember," Tom finished, "that though each one of us is important in himself, the *other* man is even more important. If we ever forget that, we fail ourselves and we fail the world of which each of us is such an important part."

A storm of applause broke out, and I sat in the rear crying silently. It was at that moment that I was sure Tom's sacrifice of our personal dreams was worthwhile. The unmarked roads that he had taken had led him right to the niche where he belonged, where he could do the most good in the world.

And every word he spoke to those students that day came right from the bottom of his heart.

7

Mixville

Sɪᴅ Jᴏʀᴅᴀɴ ᴡᴀs ɴᴏᴛ ᴏɴʟʏ Tᴏᴍ's ᴍᴏsᴛ ᴛʀᴜsᴛᴇᴅ ғʀɪᴇɴᴅ; he was also a valuable assistant to Tom in the making of his pictures.

Sid had his fair share of difficult stunts to do in Tom's pictures also.

Tom used to laugh, "I can't let myself get soft. I can't have Sid outdoing me."

No one could readily outdo Tom in any kind of physical stunt. Nor did his keen eyesight, hairspring reflexes, and faultless judgment wane as he grew older. He was, at the very end of his life, still able to vault from a horse with surprising ease; and at fifty paces he could still shoot the end off a cigar held in the smoker's mouth; and at the same distance he could split a piece of twine with unerring accuracy.

Tom was able to do all this in later years only because he

116

kept his body constantly in condition. When they were between pictures he and Sid would spend hours every day at
target practice, and on conceiving and practicing dangerous
stunts that Tom would use in later pictures. I would look
out the window of our bungalow and see them leaping all
over the yard, dodging behind trees, jumping off the porch
roof, and blasting at each other with blank cartridges.

One morning I looked out just in time to see a barrel start
its descent from our yard toward the bottom of the hill. Our
hill was steep and the barrel was soon rolling at alarming
speed toward the clump of trees at the bottom. Tom and Sid
were inside the barrel, and by the time it reached the bottom
of the hill the barrel was in splinters and Tom and Sid were
laughing hard as they rubbed their bruises and sore spots.

They used this idea in Tom's next picture. After their close-
quarter fight in a barrel, the barrel bumped down a rocky in-
cline twice as steep as the hill they had practiced on. Sid came
out of this scene unconscious, and Tom emerged with a broken bone, but the scene was so novel and effective that they
considered their efforts worthwhile.

There was the time, too, when Tom and Sid spent days
trying to perfect a chariot race stunt for one of Tom's early
Hollywood pictures. Tom was cast as a Roman gladiator in
this film, one of the few non-Westerns he made after he settled in Hollywood. He was supposed to be thrown out of a
chariot when it was rolling at full speed, but no matter how
many times he practiced the scene he still wasn't satisfied that
he was ejected from the chariot violently enough to please his
movie fans. One day he conceived the idea of tying an anvil
to his ankle with a rope. At the moment of crisis in the scene
he simply kicked the anvil out of the chariot with his foot and
his body catapulted out of the chariot as though he'd been
shot from a cannon. Tom limped for days after that scene, but
at last he was gratified with the result.

When Tom got "shot" in his films, it was usually Sid who did the shooting. Tom jokingly referred to him as "Big Chief Rifle Shot."

Tom highly appreciated the fact that Sid was as unerring a marksman as himself. Though blank cartridges were used in most scenes, sometimes real shells were used, especially in the early days, when the supply of blanks ran low. No matter whether blank or real shell was coming at him, Tom would go about his business in a movie scene perfectly confident that when the shot from Sid's gun came, it would come at precisely the right moment and would hit a prearranged target. During the long period of their working together, Sid must have shot a hundred glasses out of Tom's hand and put dozens of holes in his neckties. He was forever getting Tom behind a rock or in some almost impossible situation where Tom could blast his way out in typical Tom Mix screen fashion.

One day Tom and Sid came home from the studio laughing hard. When I pressed for an explanation, Sid said, "We had a *real* cowboy from Texas visiting at the studio today. He was spreading it around that Tom and I were just plain phonies."

I looked at Tom. Certainly, I thought, he hadn't passed *that* off with a laugh.

Tom was grinning. "He was telling everybody on the set that life on the range isn't anything like what we were doing in the scenes today."

"He said that the movies needed some *real* cowboys making pictures," Sid added. "But he went on to say that no real cowboy would waste his time in pictures. He said he knew that all the stunts we did in our films were tricks, that you sure fool the public with a camera."

I looked at Tom in astonishment. "You let him get away with that?"

"It was kinda fun listening to him scoff," Tom explained. "The crew got a kick out of it. We didn't have any real tough scenes to do today, so the fellow just kept on laughing and letting everybody know how much better *he* could do the scenes."

"And you let him get away with it?" I persisted.

"Not quite," laughed Sid. "First thing Tom did when the day's shooting was over was ask the cowboy to give us some pointers on how things *should* be done."

Dawn was beginning to break; I was already smiling. "All right. How did you reduce him to a sweat?"

"First I asked him to show me how to rope properly," Tom said. " I pointed out a peg on the stage and said I'd sure been trying to get a rope around it but hadn't been able to."

"The cowboy tried to rope the peg, but his reach was short," Sid said. "He said nobody could rope that peg from that distance—but Tom said that now that he'd studied the cowboy's fine roping technique he wanted to have a try again himself." Sid chuckled. "Tom put that rope around the peg with no trouble at all."

"I suppose the cowboy was convinced then?" I asked.

"No," said Tom. "He said he was willing to challenge any of us 'phony' cowboys to a shooting match. I figured it might be a good contest. So we got a can—and we started shooting it down a slope."

"The cowboy only missed once," said Sid.

"Yes," nodded Tom. "He was a good shot at that."

"But the clincher was when the cowboy took his last shot and couldn't see the can any more," Sid said, "Tom found the can and sent it clear out of sight—for good."

I nodded and smiled, remembering how Tom had sent a target can spinning on a prairie just a few years before—had sent it spinning after the rest of us had lost sight of it.

"Well, the cowboy wasn't looking so tall after that," said Sid. "In fact, he was kind of itchin' to take off. But Tom asked him to demonstrate the Indian-grip hold for him."

"The cowboy got taller then," Tom laughed. "I guess he figured he ought to be able to bend my arm over double without any trouble."

"He was a big guy," Sid explained, " and he sure looked like he could bulldog a steer with one arm. Well, he and Tom sat down at a table on the set. The cowboy was grinnin' hard when he and Tom locked arms. I guess he figured it'd take him about two seconds to have Tom's arm laid flat on the table. A few minutes later, after a lot of strainin' back and forth, that cowboy had the reddest face I've ever seen—and his arm was flat on the table where Tom had bent it."

"He didn't have any more to say after that," said Tom. "Just got up and took off. I don't expect we'll be seeing him again."

"No," I said. "I don't expect you will."

Tom had ridiculed the braggart cowboy simply to teach him a lesson. He never failed to take the wind out of a braggart when the opportunity presented itself, for he felt that a man revealed himself in his actions, not in his words. If his actions were good, the world could see that they were good, and talking about them was unnecessary. Tom himself never fell victim to the braggadocio he disliked so much in others, though this characteristic was an occupational disease inherent in the natures of many movie stars of his era.

I'm sure the swaggering cowboy left the studio that day completely convinced, beneath his personal humiliation, that Tom was anything but a "phony cowboy."

As for the cowboy's idea that the camera could deceive the public, he was right. The camera could be employed for deception and was, in many pictures, but never in a Tom Mix film. And this was true in spite of the fact that many of the stunts Tom did on the screen seemed virtually impossible to do. They would have been impossible for anyone else.

The forming of the Selig-Tom Mix Company placed Tom in a position of real power, a position that he could have misused had he been a different kind of man. But though Tom had virtually absolute control over all facets of the production of his film, he became no panjandrum. Except for the tension that came to him from ever-increasing responsibility, he remained unchanged.

He considered himself and the people he worked with as one big team. Before he began each picture he gathered the other actors and the production crew together for a kind of pre-filming pep talk to remind them that the Tom Mix films were by no means merely the product of the efforts of one individual.

"We have a responsibility to ourselves and to the public to make this picture as good as we possibly can," Tom would say, " and it will take *all* of us to make it that way."

His sincerity and humility reached the hearts of everyone he ever worked with. He was not merely a great star to them; he was also best friend, mentor, and hero to all of them. Consequently, the filming of a Tom Mix film usually went off without a hitch, and with a minimum of frayed nerves and an almost complete exclusion of temperament.

Things invariably went that way because the people who worked with Tom loved him and respected him. He was a thoroughly fair man in all his dealings, but he always carried with him the note of authority that had earned him such deep respect in his days as a sheriff. He seldom had to use his authority as a weapon, but when disciplinary action was necessary, he took quick but fair action.

Such an occasion arose once when we left Hollywood to do a film on location in the Arizona desert. Life in the production camp would have gone smoothly except for one thorn: the cook.

The producing of an action film on location, with its attendant hard riding over difficult terrain and the other strenuous work, makes for hearty appetites when mealtime rolls around. On this location trip appetites were at an all-time high because the working days lasted from dawn to dusk. Tom had reasoned that a double working day would bring the film to completion in half the usual time, thus giving the production crew the opportunity to get back to their families in California all the sooner. Everyone worked feverishly to attain this objective. Everyone, that is, except the cook.

The cook was a burly, sour individual, an ex-prizefighter and a dissenter from way back. He was obviously a misfit in the company of the friendly, cooperative crew that formed Tom's film unit. He throughly disliked Tom and referred to him, not quite under his breath, as a "plutocrat cowboy." His resentment crept into the meals he prepared for the company; they were not only unsavory, they were also inadequate.

Tom tried to set the cook straight by having a few talks with him. But the meals continued to be unsavory, inadequate, and unpunctual.

The climax came early one morning when the crew was scheduled to rise at three-thirty, eat breakfast and then travel to an arroyo where a special scene had to be filmed just as dawn broke.

Everyone arose on time expecting breakfast to be waiting. But it wasn't. The cook was lying sullenly on his cot in the cook tent.

Tom didn't explode. He simply walked into the tent and pulled the cook out of his cot.

The burly cook glowered at Tom. "You treat this company like a bunch of slaves," the cook said. "Three-thirty in the morning! Well, I'm not cookin' at three-thirty for—"

Tom started shaking the big ex-prizefighter-cook. Those of us standing at the entrance of the cook tent were soon being driven back by the heavy action that was going on inside.

The cook started plunging his heavy fists at Tom, who side-stepped them nicely with his usual agility. He got in a couple of quick blows to the cook's face, which brought a roar of anger from the bellicose giant. Then Tom seized the man's shoulders and started turning him around and around, getting him dizzy and winded. They swept past tables and cookstoves, and kitchenware fell to the ground with a deafening clatter. The cook spun into a corner of the tent, knocking down the supporting pole—and the tent sagged down on one side.

The cook got hold of some dispersed pots and pans and started hurling them at Tom. Tom warded them off with the cover of a garbage can, which he used as a shield.

The next thing we knew, the two men were locked together and throwing each other around the tent. In the ensuing violence the rest of the tent collapsed upon them within a few seconds. The fight continued under the flattened canvas and then, after an interminable period, there was silence.

The crew dived in and picked up the tent. There was Tom, sitting calmly on the stomach of the fallen giant, and grinning.

Tom wasted no time in getting the cook dispatched to the nearest town. There was no breakfast that morning, but the crew voted to go on with work as usual. For the duration of the location trip the cameraman's wife and I divided the cooking duties between us.

There was more than the cook-tent fight to lend excitement during the making of this film. Tom had a real-life experience while we were on this location trip that was reminiscent of some of the tight spots in which he found himself during his days as a marshal.

He rose one Sunday and said he was going to the nearest town, which was some thirty or forty miles away from our location camp, to renew his acquaintance with the sheriff, Harry Wrightman, whom he had known in his pre-movie days.

I became frantic with worry when he didn't return to camp

by evening. By the time he finally got back, some time near dawn of the next day, I was livid with anger.

"Tom Mix!" I sputtered. "I've waited all night for you! I was worried to death. I thought you might have had an accident—"

Tom looked sheepish. "I'm sorry," he said. "I wanted to send word that I'd probably be a while getting back here, but there wasn't any time. I had a job to do, Olive."

Tom told me he had arrived in town that Sunday just in time to be swept into the wave of excitement which had enveloped the town over a killing that had taken place only a few minutes before. The posse that was to ride out after the murderer was forming at the sheriff's place only a few minutes before Tom arrived.

Sheriff Harry Wrightman, just about to mount his horse, pumped Tom's hand. "Sure glad to see you, Tom," he said. "Can't stop to talk right now. Local fellow shot down an unarmed man in a fight over a horse not ten minutes ago and hightailed it out of here—"

"How about deputizing me fast, Harry," Tom suggested. "I've had a little experience tracking down murderers."

A few moments later Tom was riding out of town with the sheriff and about a dozen other men. They rode fast and hard over the desert, following the escaped murderer's trail toward a large butte that rose out of the sand a few miles to the south.

When they reached the butte a shot rang out from a cave about half way up where the murderer had taken refuge.

The men dismounted and took cover behind the boulders and rocks that fringed the base of the butte.

"You can't get out of this no matter how hard you try!" the sheriff shouted up to the trapped murderer. "We're going to stay here as long as you do—so you may as well come on down right now."

The sheriff's logic fell on unappreciative ears. The answer
from the cave was a blast of shotgun fire. Like a trapped wild
animal, the man was determined to fight it out to the end. In
his cave he held a strategic vantage point. He could see every
movement below him, but he could not be seen.

"We're not getting anywhere," announced Tom after an
hour passed. "I think I can sneak around to the back of the
butte and come on him from above without being seen. It's
worth a chance."

"It's risky," Harry said. "I can't let you go. You're too important a man for anything like that!"

Tom ignored him. "I'm going to try it. Now when I get
above him I'll signal you and you raise your hat a little above
this rock. . . ."

Tom, hugging the ground, crept cautiously along the butte,
hiding behind one rock and then wriggling along the ground
to the next one, at any moment expecting the murderer to
detect him from his surveillance point high on the face of the
butte. When he was certain he was out of range, he rose and
skirted the side of the butte, moving quickly to the rear side.

Here he hesitated. The criminal's ascent to his cave on the
face of the butte had been comparatively easy for him because of the easy slope on that side and because of the nu-
merous projections he could grip while climbing.

Tom didn't hesitate long. Foot by foot he moved up the
precipitous rear route. Several times he thought he couldn't
make it. It was a long time before he reached the top.

Cautiously he worked himself up to the face of the butte,
careful not to kick down a stone or make any other noise that
would alert the murderer to the fact that someone was coming on him from above. Tom saw that conditions below had
not changed in the long time it had taken him to accomplish
this much of his maneuver; the posse was still barricaded be-

hind the rocks below, and their victim was still watching and waiting from the dark recesses of the cave.

Silently, slowly, Tom began sliding down the face of the butte. When he had reached a point directly above the entrance of the cave, he signaled the sheriff and, as they had previously arranged, the sheriff raised his hat over the rock, as though preparing to move out to take a shot at the murderer.

As Tom had anticipated, this movement brought the outlaw forward, out of the shadows of the cave, to get a bead on his intended target. When Tom saw the man's hand appear, he swung down into the cave entrance and knocked the startled murderer over with his swinging boots.

The man groped wildly for the gun that had been flung out of his hand by the impact.

"Oh, no you don't!" yelled Tom, pouncing on the gun and flinging it out of the cave.

But this wasn't quite the finish. The disarmed man turned on Tom and fought him like a wild animal. They pounded each other with fists and then in close embrace rolled to the ledge outside. Tom, realizing the danger of the situation, managed to flip his antagonist over, grab his hand and jackknife it behind his back.

A few moments later he delivered the quarry to the posse.

"That was all there was to it," Tom said after finishing the story.

"*All?*" I said. "Tom Mix, you take enough risks in your pictures. Why do you take unnecessary chances outside when you don't have to?"

"Helping to bring a murderer to justice is everybody's business," he returned. "I had to do my part."

When Tom reigned as William Fox's biggest star in the postwar period, he had an even more elaborate organization for the production of his pictures than with Selig. Production activities were carried on at a special studio lot covering twelve acres of ground near Edendale, California. This home of Tom's Fox pictures was appropriately called Mixville. Tom was undisputed "King of Mixville," just as he was the king of the screen cowboys.

With Fox he reached the apex of his screen career. His responsibilities also increased a hundredfold. There were scores of people working with him at Mixville, each one of whom depended upon the success of the Tom Mix films as a source of livelihood.

To Tom his fellow workers comprised one big team, a team that functioned efficiently and never became unwieldy simply because he, as the captain, always had the wisdom to treat other persons as human beings.

His splendid treatment of the people he worked with resulted in increasingly better films as time went on. Productions became more elaborate, although nothing was sacrificed to action. He knew that his fans wanted action above everything else—and that's what he gave them. Every new picture came out with new stunts, each more dangerous than previous ones.

Many of the interior scenes were made at Mixville. Almost everything pertaining to the Old West could be found tucked away somewhere in this unique little settlement; indeed, the vast lot was a miniature West in itself. There was a complete frontier town, with a dusty street, hitching rails, a saloon, jail, bank, doctor's office, surveyor's office, and the simple frame houses typical of the early Western era. Only the signs on the buildings were changed from picture to picture, and some rearrangement of the furnishings.

There was an Indian village with several lodges nestled in a flat piece of land at the rear of the lot. From the range of plaster-of-Paris mountains surrounding the village Tom led many a convincing attack on a tribe of warriors, the whole

thing looking ferociously real when the picture reached the
screen.

There was a plot of simulated desert too, through which
Tom and Tony wandered on many an occasion on their
search for the "bad man"; for although Tom preferred actual
locations, the Fox executives always held the budget over his
head.

Among other things at Mixville there were a ranch house,
sans any ceiling of course, a corral that would hold a hundred
horses, and a great barnlike structure to hold props, such as
saddles, uniforms, guns, and various items of furniture that
conformed to the Old West tradition.

This big organization that Tom ruled over at Mixville was
a complicated business. The executives were fully aware that
Tom's judgment was canny and that he, more than anyone
else, was best interpreting what the public wanted, and incidentally more profitable to the William Fox Company. So
Tom carried on with practically no restrictions. He planned his
films from start to finish, even to writing large chunks of many
scripts. He was an expert director, a competent producer, and
a master at seeing that his films, in their unified whole, were as
effective as possible.

When he wasn't actually working on the lot, Tom could
usually be found conferring with his assistants at the main
studio located at the junction of Western Avenue and Sunset
Boulevard in Hollywood. He also had an office and a dressing
room there, as well as a private gymnasium. He never rested
for a moment; he even held conferences in his dressing room
when he was between scenes of a picture, or in the gym.

Mixville itself was just as much a symbol of his greatness as
were the films that emerged as the finished product from its
twelve acres. And he almost lost his life trying to save the little studio town on one fateful day.

It was a Sunday afternoon, when only Tom and a half dozen other men were on the lot. A fire broke out in the livery stable that served as one of the buildings in the frontier town set. Tom spied the conflagration from the window of his office where he was holding a conference with the director and a few of the technical men regarding the next day's shooting schedule.

"Come on, men!" Tom shouted, jumping up and leaping out of the window. That was the shortest route to the stable, where were quartered seven or eight horses, the overflow from the regular horse barns.

The fire gathered force quickly. By the time Tom reached the structure it was thick with smoke, and the horses were whinnying in terror. Tom rushed in and, by the time the other men arrived, he was leading out the first horse.

Getting a horse from a burning building is a difficult task. Nothing will throw a horse into a panic more quickly than fire. A horse will resist human efforts to save its life only when it is afraid, and leading a skittish animal from a burning stable is a strenuous task.

With the help of the other men there was only one horse left in the stable when the fire had reached the point where it seemed impossible to do anything. But Tom went back into the inferno and brought out the last horse just before the building collapsed. He was taken to the hospital for treatment of his burns, but he was back on the lot the following morning.

8

The Summit

Tom's insurrections didn't come often because of Tom's conscientious attitude toward his place in the world. But they came to him, as they come to all persons of fame, when the pressures squeezed in too hard from all directions.

The first bit of personal insurrection came shortly after we were married. There was another kind of pressure on Tom then: the one brought about by being married very suddenly after a life of complete freedom on the Western ranges. It burst in him one afternoon shortly after we returned to Oklahoma following our honeymoon.

"I think I'll take the team and ride in to Bartlesville and talk to some of the boys this afternoon," he told me.

"All right," I said, "but remember, we're having guests for supper and the evening."

Tom left for Bartlesville in my beautiful new rubber-tired

buggy, a vehicle which was the last word in Western luxury in those days. My most prized horses, a team of perfectly
matched bay thoroughbreds, were pulling the buggy.

Suppertime arrived, but no Tom. I fidgeted uncomfortably
throughout the meal. I did some even heavier fidgeting during the rest of the evening. By the time our guests finally acknowledged to themselves that they weren't going to be able
to meet Tom that evening, I had felt the symptoms of high
blood pressure for the first time in my young life.

At eleven o'clock I sat on the porch waiting. At midnight I
was still waiting. At two o'clock I heard the familiar fast
clomping of hoofs on the road, and a moment later Tom tore
through the gate in the buggy. He swung it madly in an arc
around the house and then headed toward the corral. His
six-shooter rang out a salute in the stillness of the night.

Under the brightness of the full moon I watched from my
vantage point on the porch as Tom reined up and jumped out
of the buggy. The throughbreds, completely keyed up from
their frantic run, weren't at rest for more than a moment.
Before Tom could stop them they were plunging the empty
buggy through a partly excavated cellar. The buggy was
wrenched loose from the horses as they leaped out the other
end, and with bits of harness flying, they tore out the front
gate to be lost until noon of the following day.

Tom came slowly toward the porch. When he was a few feet
away from me he sensed that it was time to stop.

"Hello, Olive," he said weakly, trying frantically to smile.

I was in no mood to be smiled at. I raised my arm and
showed him that I was holding in my hand a .30-.30 Winchester.

"Find yourself a tree, Tom," I said briskly.

"Now, Olive," he remonstrated.

I raised the Winchester higher. "You'd better find that tree
right now," I said.

I must have looked as menacing as I felt for Tom turned, ran, and was hidden behind a tree in the yard by the time I let go my first blast of the Winchester.

A moment later his head appeared from behind the tree. "Listen, dear," he called out.

I emptied the Winchester again.

This went on for something like an hour before I finally set aside the rifle and let him withdraw from behind his shelter.

He came up to the porch looking very contrite.

"Olive, I don't blame you for doing this," he said. "Now that the steam's out of both of us, we're better off for it. I don't know why I stayed on in Bartlesville tonight when I knew you were waiting here. I just don't know why."

I didn't know why, either, for a long time. When this episode occurred I was still far too young to understand that Tom's nature had been carved so deeply in his free days that his past would keep popping out in him repeatedly when the pressures of his new worlds tightened on him. It was something that those persons closest to him in his life grew to see clearly in him. It was something that he himself never quite understood.

In the late twenties there was a different kind of insurrection. On this occasion Tom, for the first time in his entire screen career, held up production on a picture because he momentarily lost contact with his deep basic strength, the strength that had daily prompted him to do his job for the world despite any personal troubles that were bothering him.

He simply disappeared from Mixville one day right in the midst of a picture, although later in the day he did call up his faithful secretary at the main studio in Hollywood and tell her he was going out of town. That was all he said to her; then he hung up.

A search was instigated for him at once, but two days

dragged by without any word from him and without the discovery of a trace of evidence as to where he might have gone. He was so famous by then that he was recognized immediately no matter where he went; hence his mysterious disappearance was all the more amazing.

At home I waited and waited for a telephone call from Tom. Though he and I had been divorced for some time by then, I knew he would call when the force of pressure became too great for him.

Finally the call came.

"I'm at Lake Arrowhead," Tom said. His voice was edged with strain. "Can—Ruth come up here?"

I swallowed hard, as I recognized that tone of anxiety from the past.

"Of course Ruth can come up there," I assured him. "You just sit tight, Tom."

Ruth was in her early teens then, but in understanding her father she was far in advance of her years. She left immediately for Lake Arrowhead. Later she told me every detail of her visit with her father.

When she got there she found him in a state of deep doldrums. He had lost several pounds almost overnight.

"What's the matter, Daddy?" Ruth asked upon entering the cabin he had rented. "You aren't sick, are you?"

Tom thumped the region of his heart. "Just sick here, Ruthie."

She sat down beside him and put her arms around him.

"Now tell me all about it, Daddy. There are a lot of people waiting for you back at Mixville—and millions of others waiting for that picture that is half finished."

Tom got up and paced around the cabin. "I really don't know what's the matter, Ruthie," he said. "All of a sudden I got fed up on everything. I didn't want to see anybody. I wanted to forget that I was Tom Mix, the famous movie star—just be all by myself and have a chance to think."

"That makes sense," Ruth told him. "Everybody in the limelight has the same feeling once in a while. Most of them don't do anything about it. I'm glad you did. Now you can go back and feel a lot better."

Under Ruth's persuasive philosophy Tom brightened up. "Come on, Ruthie!" he exclaimed. "Let's go!"

Probably few people realize the enormous strain put upon a famous person. No doubt every single one of them would give anything in the world to go away sometimes and just be utterly alone for a while.

The decade of the twenties was the period of maturity for the silent film. It was also the period of fabulous business success in Hollywood. And it was the period of the vamp, of big Hollywood money, of Hollywood scandals.

It was, too, the big period of Tom's fame. When Tom started at Fox he had agreed to a contract calling for a fairly low basic salary plus a percentage of the profits from his pictures. At that time neither Tom nor the studio expected his films to be as enormously successful as they turned out to be.

It was soon evident that Tom was to Fox what John Gilbert was to Metro-Goldwyn-Mayer and Gloria Swanson to Paramount. He was the foremost box-office attraction in America for years despite the fact that his pictures—always films of simple structure and generally made on a comparatively low budget—were too unsophisticated to be booked for the long runs in the big city motion picture palaces that the more spectacular films enjoyed. The roots of Tom's fame were planted in the thousands of small towns in America where the advent of a new Tom Mix picture was always heralded by youngsters as a major event in their lives.

He was always highly conscious of his tremendous influence

on the youth of the world. He was their mentor of clean living, and his message to youth was: "Take care of your body, keep your mind clean, and always be truthful." It was the dictum he followed in his personal mode of living.

And the youth of the world responded to him with uninhibited enthusiasm. Fan letters streamed in daily by the thousands, and every letter was acknowledged. Tom employed two secretaries to handle his regular fan mail and a special secretary to handle requests from parents who wanted Tom to write individual messages of encouragement to their children.

A day never slipped by without Tom's receipt of hundreds of letters of appreciation from parents, praising him for supplying their children with the moral type of picture that would be helpful to molding their future lives.

"I know I've got a reputation to live up to," he once told a press agent. "I *want* to be a good influence on the young people who follow me. I never want to disappoint them. So I've got to live up to what they expect of me." He smiled. "For a long time that used to bother me. I thought I might be missing a lot of fun. I couldn't go places where sometimes I wanted to go, because I was sure the kids wouldn't like it. I felt sort of hedged in. But I changed my mind about that pretty fast . . . after I realized that I really wanted to lead the life the kids expected me to lead."

It was these simple action films that made Tom's name a household word. Through his help and willingness to take a chance on them, such famous stars as Barbara LaMarr, Colleen Moore, Billie Dove, Clara Bow, Laura LaPlante, and Ann Pennington, at one time or another gained prestige as the pure white heroines that graced Tom's films.

The wall that rose between Tom and me was the product of the conflict that dwelled within him: the struggle between the personality of the movie star and the man of the plains.

We decided on divorce simply because our life together couldn't be what we had so long wanted it to be—what it had started out to be. It was far too late for that. The incompatibility between us did not grow from within our house, but from the forces that beat upon it from the outside. Our separation was not one of bitterness, but one of deep sadness.

Consequently I stood on the sidelines to watch Tom's growing incandescence in the twenties—and to glory with him. Always I prayed that he would be preserved to continue to bring happiness to the world. He was the father of my child, and in the depth of his love for Ruth I found happiness. I was proud that he never became obsessed with his power and did not succumb to ego fever. His name remained spotless when the Hollywood scandals of the early twenties rocked the world.

Tom amazed an interviewer once by pulling out a much-thumbed-through book that he referred to as "The Hollywood Graveyard." It was actually a collection of short biographies of every important person who had been connected with the motion picture business.

"Out of the hundreds of names in this book," Tom told the interviewer, "there are only four who are still active in the industry. You know why? Some of them drank themselves out. Some of them were crooked. Others felt they were better than the public that paid to see them, and *acted* that way. Then there were others who thought they were smarter than the producers who were trying to guide their careers." Tom paused. "I guess you could go over this list of names and find just about every reason for human failure there is. I like to go over it when I get to feeling a little too big for my britches. It makes a man think."

Tom consistently ignored the Hollywood women, although there were at most points in his career a number of them running after him. His gentleness, his concern for people, his full-blown personality and virile good looks made him a natural target for the lonely women who came to Hollywood to try to enter pictures. He repeatedly squelched the attempts of these women to ensnare him. But on one occasion when an "amateur vamp" persisted in pestering him, he gave Hollywood something to laugh about for a long time.

The woman had enjoyed a very brief and minor prominence on the screen as a vampish type of actress. Tom was the "tall, dark and handsome" type of man for which she yearned. She kept calling him at Mixville to invite him to join her for cocktails at her house in the Hollywood Hills.

To her surprise, Tom accepted one of her invitations. When he arrived, she launched immediately into the siren act she had performed with some success on the screen.

Tom let her go on and then started laughing. He could never stand affected people, persons who attitudinized every waking moment. He decided to teach this particular vamp a lesson. He advanced toward her with two drapery ropes that he tore from the windows.

"What are you going to do?" she shrieked.

"I'm going to hang you up to dry," Tom said.

While the woman screamed, Tom bound her with the ropes and then made a sort of hammock out of a piece of cloth he found. He settled the enraged woman in the improvised hammock and tied it to the chandelier. Then he made an anonymous telephone call to the police after he had left the house and told them to go to the vamp's address, where they would find her in an embarrassing situation.

When the police arrived and cut her down from her perch, she concocted a story about how some burglars had tied her up. The true story came out later, however, and all Hollywood got a big laugh out of it.

Tom had many, many friends in Hollywood, just as he had everywhere else he lived during his life. His Hollywood friends included none of the riotous livers, those few stars who painted a false picture of Hollywood with their wild public shenanigans. It was these few who made people think that Hollwood was something approaching a continuous Babylonian orgy. Tom's friends were among the quiet people of Hollywood who actually composed the biggest part of the Hollywood scene.

Though the basic qualities of Tom's character never changed, there were changes in his mode of living that came as a natural result of his fame and success, changes that even affected his personality and at times turned him into a man of extremes.

His extravagance became almost a disease. There was the great mansion in Beverly Hills, for instance, to which he had come from a simple stucco cottage where he had lived during the first few years he was in Hollywood. When he moved into this pretentious structure he brought with him hundreds of trophies of contest and achievement that had almost filled the stucco cottage: countless ornamental saddles and silver-encrusted bridles; an arsenal of rifles and revolvers; his enormous collection of spurs, sombreros, ribbons, medals and loving cups. These trophies, all manifestations and symbols of his past life—the life that he was constantly reaching back to look for—were egregiously out of place among the expensive pieces of imported furniture and the carefully conceived decorations of the new home.

The mansion was set on a knoll in the center of a six-acre, walled-in estate crowded with elaborate formal gardens that required the constant attention of a corps of gardeners. There was a seven-car garage that housed at various times from $75,000 to $100,000 worth of automobiles.

There was a special stable for Tony, almost a house in itself.

Tom's initials were everywhere. The T-M brand appeared on the huge electrically controlled front gate, on the doors of the house, over every fireplace, on almost every piece of equipment he owned.

This residence was a manifestation of his extravagance, the ultimate symbol of success achieved; and yet he was not completely happy amid all of the luxury. Once he commented to an interviewer that the place made him tremendously lonely, even among a score of servants and a continuous parade of visitors.

Maybe it was a way of life that he had entered into because of some spiritual loneliness . . . a seeking to find a substitute for something missing . . . a deep inner need that was not being fulfilled. When he disposed of the house in later years he did so without regret.

He was extravagant in his business investments too. He put many of his old friends into business, expecting no return and usually not getting any. He purchased almost a million dollars in stocks and securities that became worthless when the stock market plummeted in 1929. His real estate investments ran into the hundreds of thousands; most of the properties had been bought at inflated prices and later were worth only a fraction of what he paid for them. He financed a wildcat oil project and lost over a half million in the transaction.

His extravagance extended to his clothing, which had been more or less an obsession with him from youth and which he now was able to indulge to his heart's content: flamboyant, colorful outfits, business suits trimmed with leather; sports jackets that were so loud they screamed to high heaven. He had always enjoyed bright, happy colors and said they were a tonic to him.

Then there were the brilliant cowboy hats and gaily decorated, hand-tooled boots. And diamonds! The big diamond that Tom purchased for me in Montana would have been utterly lost among the diamond stickpins, shirt studs, tiepins, rings, wrist watches he accumulated—even one pair of diamond-studded spurs! Maybe Tom could not compete with Diamond Jim Brady, but he came a close second.

Naturally it was the thing for movie stars to have a yacht, and so Tom had one. I've never met anyone, however, who saw him on the vessel after a few weeks following his purchase of it. Tom was not and never had been a "salt water" man. His soul was in the plains, the prairies and deserts.

His automobiles, one of which was to carry the specter of Death in the rear seat, were specially built for him. They were the biggest, sportiest and highest powered that could be acquired at that time. If a more flamboyant one was obtainable in Europe, Tom would order it. His exuberance spilled over into fast, reckless driving which more than once landed him in a hospital.

And at last in 1921 Tom bought that "dream ranch" in Arizona. As he had always wanted, it was an enormous place— thousands of acres of grazing land . . . hills . . . gullies . . . streams . . . everything! But there was no one who really loved him to share it with him. Those who were believed to be closest to him would have none of it. Where could he find anyone to trade the glamor of Beverly Hills for a life on the lonely plains? So it was only on rare occasions that he visited the ranch, and he soon turned over its entire supervision to others.

The time came when Tom thought of retiring, but the world had grown to love him too much to permit it. An avalanche of protest in the form of thousands of letters from all over the world convinced him that he had a role in life which in fairness to his youthful worshipers he could not relinquish.

He continued giving his vast public a generous quota of films every year. In 1926 the titles of his films were emblazoned around the world: *The Yankee Señor, Tony Runs Wild, My Own Pal, Hardboiled, The Great K and A Robbery, The Canyon of Light,* and *No Man's Gold.* In 1927 he made *The Last Trail, Bronco Twister, The Outlaws of Red River, Circus Ace, Tumbling River, Silver Valley,* and *Arizona Wildcat.* In 1928: *The Devil's Reward, A Horseman of the Plains, Hello, Cheyenne, The Painted Post, A Son of the Golden West,* and an especially big hit—*Coming of the Law.*

Tom's films in the twenties were simply enlargements of the basic structure that had made his early two-reelers so successful. They consisted of plenty of action, a simple plot, a very white hero, an impossibly incorrigible villain, a number of dangerous schemes to be foiled, and a helpless heroine to be rescued at the last moment. It was a formula that did not fail to delight his public for many, many years.

He checked constantly on the effect of his films on the public, and maintained a card index of notations concerning the public opinion expressed of his pictures. He wrote frequently to clergymen to verify that his pictures were not detrimental to the millions of his youthful fans. He was his own personal censor.

"This won't do," he once told a writer, who had fashioned a script that he felt was novel and refreshing. "You've got me smoking, gambling, and drinking—and it won't do."

The script writer was taken aback. "I was only trying to get away from the old formula," he explained.

"The kids wouldn't understand," Tom answered. "You see, I can't do anything the boys and girls don't expect of me. The story of the West is of big interest to the youth of the world—and they've come to associate me with that story. I've heard that a lot of kids even imitate me. Now do you understand why this script won't do?"

The writer was a little hesitant. "Well, I still think it's a good script."

"Sure," said Tom. "It'll be swell when we cut out some things. The role I play on the screen has got to represent a man of high ideals. Just remember that when you do the script over, then we'll come out all right on it. We've got to convince the boyhood of America that drinking and gambling are bad, that physical fitness always wins out over dissipation, that a good life brings rewards and evildoing brings punishment."

In revising the script, the writer remembered those things and the picture turned out to be one of the best Tom ever made.

It was seldom that Tom deviated from his formula. He never turned to the "modernized" Western. In later years, in an effort to achieve novelty, many cowboy stars turned aviators in their films and mixed the old Western with modern thrills. Tom refused to resort to this device. He kept to the plains and the mountains; he used stagecoaches, Indians, and bad men. He held to the Old West to the end of his film career.

In 1929 he made a personal appearance tour with Tony which was an enormous success. But in 1929, when the big changeover to talking pictures began, he made only three films: *Outlawed*, *The Big Diamond Robbery*, and *The Drifter*.

Like a great many other stars, he was skeptical about what talking pictures might do to him. He decided to retire from the screen and accept an offer to appear with the Sells-Floto Circus.

9

The Big Top

Tom SPENT THE SEASONS OF 1929, 1930 AND 1931 AS THE star of the Sells-Floto Circus. These were three of the most successful years of his life and they were extremely happy for him, for the reception to his act was overwhelming everywhere the circus played.

His association with Sells-Floto brought him twenty thousand dollars a week and a private railroad car to travel in. There was a private railroad car for Tony too. There were servants to cater to Tom's every need. He enjoyed every possible luxury the circus could afford.

But these weren't the things that gave him deep satisfaction during this period. His happiness came mostly from the thrill he received from playing to live audiences. It was far more gratifying to him to play directly to the people, as he did in the circus, than from a rather remote position on the screen. It gave him a kind of electric response to know that the big top was jammed with people waiting in suspense for his glittering entrance and performance.

Invariably, before every performance, he would say to the equestrian director: "We've got to be just a little better to-day than we were yesterday—all of us—because we've got more to give today than we had yesterday."

The enthusiastic response to his act—which manifested itself in tumultuous cheering and resulted more than once in a wave of fans breaking from the stands and literally engulfing him in the center ring when he finished his act—was like an elixir to him. He kept striving for a higher degree of perfection and he achieved it, in spite of the fact that he had to do his circus riding with one shoulder held together by wire. The injuries he had suffered to his spine also caused him periods of agonizing pain. But the spectators were completely unaware of what he had to undergo at times. When he was in the saddle he was radiant, and this radiance seized the spectators and washed right back to him like a tidal wave.

Though Tom was in his early fifties, he had lost none of his litheness, grace and facility of movement, nor any of the magnetic qualities that had made him a star in the first place. Whenever he was acting, he was vibrant and alive, utterly oblivious to any physical handicaps. It was an amazing demonstration of the power of the mind and the will to do.

His grand entry tour around the hippodrome track prior to his trick riding and shooting acts was a sustained five minutes of cheering. His eyes seemed to be on everyone; his smile seemed to encompass everyone. The brilliant outfit he wore flashed out at the audience and the shining ornaments on Tony dazzled the spectators' eyes.

After his slow entry turn around the hippodrome track was

finished, he would spurt Tony into a gallop. They raced around the track leaping hurdles and skirting obstacles with the same fire they had shown on the screen. He vaulted in and out of the saddle and leaned down until his head was close to the ground. He leaped and tumbled on horseback, alternating fork jumps with perfect jump-ups. His was absolutely the high achievement in gymnastic horsemanship.

During the last turn around the track Tom drew his six-shooter and, at high gallop, shot at and unfailingly brought down three targets perched at difficult angles in the tent rigging. The climax of this act brought a roar of appreciation from the spectators.

Dismounted in the center ring, Tom shot at and shattered with incredible speed and accuracy a volley of colored glass balls that an assistant kept throwing into the air. He shot at targets from every conceivable angle and position. He would, for example, lean over and shoot between his legs; or roll in a somersault and come up shooting; or hold up a mirror and shoot over his shoulder. He never missed.

If there ever had been any doubts among his followers that he had performed all the seemingly impossible tricks he had done on the screen, they were entirely dispelled when they saw Tom's skillful live performance.

Always of an inventive mind, he kept adding new tricks—just as he had done when making pictures. One big trick he initiated in his lasso act the second season was his simultaneous roping of six cowgirls riding side by side in Roman parallel at high speed.

Every day he always had time to sign autographs for the hundreds of fans who came seeking them before and after every performance. He gave countless talks to various youth groups in the cities where the circus played, as well as many charity performances at hospitals. His special expression of charity went to crippled children. He devoted hours of his valuable time to giving thousands of them joy with the special shows he enacted for them. His financial contributions to charitable institutions were astronomical.

Though he lived in the luxury of a private railroad car, he took his meals with the crew and the other performers in the cook tent. The door of his car was always open to his friends and to anyone in need of counsel or help.

His happiest moment came, however, when Ruth joined him in the show during the 1931 season. She was only nineteen then, but she could hold her own with the best in her trick roping and shooting skills. Tom was the proudest man on earth when she appeared in his act with him. The stimulus of her presence gave him the power to display his greatest performances of all time during that season.

By the time Ruth was six years old the effects of her heritage were very much in evidence. Her daddy hadn't dubbed her his little cowgirl in vain. She grew to be slender and lithe, graceful and beautiful—the finest product of her father's life. And she became more and more proficient with horse, lasso, rifle and six-shooter. Tom taught her every trick she grew to know, and she displayed them with great competence in later years when she appeared in the Tom Mix Circus, and at the World's Fair in New York City in 1939.

Tom adored Ruth from the moment she was born. It was an adoration that continued in full intensity—and was thoroughly reciprocated—throughout Tom's life.

There was never a question of divided loyalties for Ruth after Tom and I were divorced. At a very early age she understood the real meaning of her father's place in the world, that he belonged more to the world than he did to us. And she also understood his love.

He saw her whenever he could. Given one free moment of his breathtakingly busy days, he would use that moment to call or visit her. Even when he was away on personal appearance and circus tours he never failed to reach her by telephone almost every day.

Tom's big mistake was in leaving his secure niche in the motion picture world to form his own circus. He could have gone right on making pictures, for in the 1930's the success of his early talking films proved that his screen popularity had not faded a bit. But his highly successful seasons with the Sells-Floto Circus had their effect on him. As he explained to a studio executive when he turned down a United Artists proposal to renew his contract: "I think I'll try the circus again. It gets me closer to people."

So he decided to give up making pictures on a regular basis, and made only a smattering of them after the middle 1930's. His life was centered thereafter in his circus, a venture that was to bring him heartbreak and almost destroy his spirit.

Perhaps there was another, even more personal, reason for Tom's decision to make a break from film-making. Being human, he was sensitive to the possibility of his screen popularity fading, for he had seen the same thing happen many, many times to other stars, and he wanted to finish his job on the screen in a final burst of glory, just as he had finished the other jobs he undertook in life.

I didn't realize that this fear existed in Tom until he came to visit us one day in the late 1920's. I noticed immediately that he was nervous. He was braiding a whip as he paced restlessly around the room. I recognized from these symptoms that Tom had a real problem on his mind.

"What's wrong?" I asked.

He continued pacing and didn't look at me at first. "Do you think it's time I bow out of pictures?" he said finally.

"Oh, *no*, Daddy!" Ruth exclaimed. She ran up to him and

embraced him. It was a tonic that he needed at the moment.

Tom looked at me. "Maybe they're getting a little tired of me. Maybe I'd better get out now while I'm still on top."

I looked at him with disbelief. "All right, tell us," I said. "What's happened to make you talk like this?"

He kept on pacing again, with Ruth trailing along, her hand in his. "The studio's considering a second series of Westerns to supplement mine," Tom said. "They're going to star a young fellow who's been an extra in my company for quite a while. His name is Buck Jones." Tom frowned. "I wonder what it means, Olive?"

I didn't hesitate. "It simply means that the studio feels there's room for *two* cowboy series," I said firmly. "There's plenty of room for both you and Buck Jones."

As it turned out, Buck Jones did become a great cowboy screen star; but he did not displace Tom, and there would have been plenty of room for both of them.

Tom's reign as a screen star covered more than a quarter of a century, longer than that of any other top cowboy star. His worry that the public would tire of him was never fulfilled. When he left films, it was of his own accord. He chose a particularly bad time to make this move, however, for the country was in the depths of the Great Depression, but the Depression was one reason he made the move.

He had lost a great amount of money in the stock market crash, and although he recouped some of this with his large earnings from Sells-Floto, an extensive loss from a large-scale oil production investment and serious depreciation of his real estate holdings again reduced his bank account. During this period, too, a great many of Tom's friends needed help. His money flowed to them freely and even his income from pictures wasn't sufficient to take up the slack.

He tried to explain his decision to me. "Sells-Floto made a

big profit, even though bad times had already started," he said. "I can't see any real reason why my own circus shouldn't make a profit, can you, Olive?"

"No," I said, because I knew he had made up his mind anyway; but I did feel a premonition of disaster.

"I've got enough capital to get it started," he said, "and given a few breaks it should do all right." He smiled. "And a few of my old friends need jobs too. This will kind of give them a break."

I had thought as much. Tom never started any kind of venture from purely selfish motives.

He paced around. "These bad times make it rough on everyone. People need entertainment now more than ever. They need to be thrilled and given a chance to laugh. They must have fun now. It's important to a person's psychology in these bad times." He smacked his fist against his palm. "We'll charge the lowest admission charge we can make ends meet on, and we'll give them the best show possible to offer."

"I know you'll do that," I said. "Tom, I have some money I can invest, if it will help." My oil royalties were still coming in regularly from the Oklahoma ranch.

He looked at me and smiled. "I knew I could count on you to help. But no, thanks, not this time. It's just too risky for you."

I knew then that he too foresaw an edge of blackness around his rosy dream.

There are an infinite number of things that can go wrong in a circus venture. It is first of all a terribly expensive undertaking. There is a tremendous amount of equipment to be purchased and maintained. Performers have to be fed, housed, moved, and paid. Animals must be cared for. There are countless problems to be faced every day. And there is the eternal bugaboo—the weather—to be faced. A week of bad weather can eat up all the profits a circus makes in a month of bland weather.

Even as these words are being written, that "Greatest Show on Earth"—Ringling Brothers—has given up fighting the disasters and hardships attendant upon a road show. But those valiant circus people will never be forgotten and there will be a great void for new generations. It is saddening when one thinks of the joy and excitement the circus gave to us as children. Some of the most thrilling moments of my youth were spent in watching the "big tent" being erected . . . entering into a new and fascinating world filled with strange animals . . . the smell of sawdust . . . the band players with their natty red jackets and gold buttons . . . the clowns carrying on their antics. . . . As these memories return, probably I understand now more than I did then why Tom loved the circus.

The year Tom organized his circus was a bad year for all circuses. Economic illness had pervaded all businesses deeply and had touched upon the entertainment world with particular impact. Even such almost unshakable organizations as Barnum and Bailey and Ringling Brothers were faltering badly.

Tom spent all his available capital getting the show organized and went to every extreme to see that the show was perfect. Though his own act was the star attraction, he hired aerialists, bareback riders, equestriennes, and clowns to fill out the program and make certain there was something for everyone's taste. He engaged high-salaried artists and retained Johnny Agee as equestrian director. Johnny had formerly served in that capacity with Barnum and Bailey and Ringling Brothers. He was a top man in the field. He and Tom together organized a first-class show.

All the elements for success were there, but the bad luck began almost at once.

Tom's funds were exhausted by the time his circus moved out of its training quarters to play its first engagement. There was a wave of excitement among the performers and the crew as they moved by truck, bus, car and trailer toward the first town. Eevryone was confident that a circus starring Tom Mix just couldn't fail. But Tom himself was worried. Unless the circus had immediate success he would find it difficult to meet the first week's payroll. Anything could happen. And it did.

Upon arrival in the first town Tom and his people were faced with a sickening sight; a flat gray sheet of rain, a torrent of it, which didn't stop, just went on and on. The circus grounds were a sleazy bog. Trucks and buses were soon up to their hubs in the miry ooze. It was the most discouraging sight Tom had faced since his black experience at the Western Washington Fair Grounds many years before.

Still, the show *had* to go on.

By the time the rain had abated for awhile, however, the damage was done. The ooze was deep. Erecting the big top in such bogging circumstances was a gargantuan task. Tom and the performers pitched in to help the canvasmen. They managed to get the tent up by the time the performance hour neared, but to little avail, for the rain had resumed its steady downpour by then and very few people were able or willing to battle through it for the first night's performance. The opening night didn't go well either, for the horses couldn't perform properly. Even the thick layer of straw covering the mud did not give the ground enough firmness to allow the show to proceed at anything approaching a fast clip. The action was cut in half.

Tom didn't reveal his discouragement to his people. After the show was over he congratulated them for doing such a fine job in such difficult circumstances. Then he and Johnny Agee went to Tom's trailer, where Tom immediately started munching on a piece of celery and drank buttermilk, a nightly ritual with him before he went to bed.

"Get some sleep," he told Johnny. "Tomorrow it will be better. It has to be."

But tomorrow wasn't better. And neither was the next day or the next. It rained almost continuously while Tom's circus played in that town. The enormous expenses kept mounting; and there were no profits to offset them. Matters worsened even more when the circus was stranded in the town and couldn't meet its next playing date in time because the flooded conditions of outlying roads prevented movement of the motor caravan.

When they arrived at their next town it was pay day.

Tom called the performers and the crew together in a special meeting and gave them the details. "We've got enough for only half pay this week," he said. "I hope by next week we can make up the balance from this week's profits. If we can't, I'll get a loan from my bankers."

There was no dissension at that moment. Tom's word was unquestionable. Many of his friends were among the crew; and the rest of the people he had hired for the circus had grown to love and admire him just as had all the other persons who had worked with him.

But among the canvas crew was a troublemaker, a good man with oratory, who was soon bruiting it around that the show was doomed, that anyone in his right mind should demand his full salary right now or quit.

Not many people listened to him, but some did. A sort of creeping hysteria shuddered through the circus personnel. Suppose Tom couldn't get that loan? Suppose the week's profits were down? What if they were hit with another streak of bad luck right away? Circus people are invariably superstitious and they believe that catastrophe travels in groups of three.

Besides, in this period of economic unrest, everyone felt insecure. Money was very important to their sense of well-being; the thought of losing even a tiny part of a salary was enough to make for worry.

The alarm among the personnel grew steadily that week, for the box office was poor. Again it was rain—enormous quantities of it—that kept the customers away. Rain, the bane of any circus, seemed to be following Tom's circus around like a hound dog.

Pay day arrived again. Even though salaries were small in those days, the total payroll was large because of the many persons involved in putting on even a small circus. Besides the performers, there were the hostlers, the cage boys, the animal trainers, the property men, ring-stock men, black-smiths, electricians, canvasmen, roustabouts, and the cook tent people to consider.

Tom had a big problem to face that night. He was aware of the talk that the troublemaking canvasman had spread around. He knew that even his best friends were somewhat jarred by it—as everyone is when economic security is threatened.

Tom called the performers and crew together again. "First of all," he said, "we'll lay the cards out flat. We didn't make enough profit this week to pay the balance due you on last week's salaries, let alone anything on this week's. And the loan from my bankers hasn't come through yet."

There was a murmur of discontentment from the assembly.

"I can't even promise that the loan will come through," Tom said. "With money so tight, banks can't take big risks, either. But I'm sure we're going to get through this as long as we all work together. You know I can't do this without you. I don't think we can fail. What do you think?"

The nervousness among the circus personnel gradually gave way to a wave of smiles. Some of them had expected Tom to fire the troublemaker, but instead of doing so and thus inflaming suspicions that the circus might be doomed, he ignored the man, and inspired his people to have confidence in him.

"I promise you'll get paid in full," Tom said, "no matter what happens."

Even in Tom's blackest days, when he had almost completely lost trust in himself, he was able to inspire confidence in others.

It was a quality that was largely responsible for his success in the first decade of the century when he served as a marshal in several Western communities. His wiseness and ability to create confidence stood him in far greater stead than his fast draw with a gun.

Gambling was a big problem during all stages of Western development. The miner, after spending weeks of hard labor dredging his reward, would go to town and lose all the product of his work to the nearest cardsharp. The cowboy, too, after a month of solitude and monotony on the ranch, generally took his pay to town for an outburst of exuberance which usually included a try at the gaming tables.

Brawls and even death were the results of many gambling sessions. Liquor, which the cowboys called "tangleleg" because it did exactly that to them, and gambling were the scourges of early Western life. Their effects on the population were much more devastating than any of the rigors of Western living proved to be. Yet tangleleg and gambling existed and flourished because they were a form of release that the lonely men of the ranges demanded.

The gambling situation was particularly bad in Dewey, Oklahoma. The city council demanded that Tom, as city marshal, drive every element of gambling out of the community. He had already driven out the itinerant cardsharps, but the council wanted a clean sweep made of the local talent too.

"We've already forbidden gambling by law," Tom told the council, "and that hasn't worked. Personally I believe that some men have to gamble. If we get too tough on them, we'll drive them under cover, and that'll make it all the harder for us to root out the swindlers."

The council asked for his plan.

"I think we should designate a few men to run games—good honest men," he told them. "We can watch them and keep them under control. Then if there's any trouble or any evidence of cheating, we'll know where to pin the blame. Besides, we can fine the gamblers for breaking the law and use some of the gambling profits to help build schools. If we control it, we have everything to gain. It's going to go on anyway, people being human."

The council decided to adopt Tom's plan. It worked. Daily life was all the more tranquil at Dewey after that, and the gambling fines helped pay for many a public building.

Tom's dealings with other people were always prudent and wise. He was able to communicate to them the bigger aspects of things. He was a natural leader, and people had faith in him.

Before Tom's circus played its final performance it was subjected to practically all the hazards of circus life: storms, floods, wrecks, fires, blowdowns, and heartaches. It was very hard for him during this period. Besides his financial worries, he was shouldering the double burden of being the star of his circus and its managing director. He felt his responsibilities keenly, and though his troubles had a deep effect on him he kept all his inner turmoil hidden from those he worked with.

The circus personnel suffered no ultimate financial misfortune. Tom himself did, however. Before the circus died, he lost his ranch in Arizona and all his money, and was forced to go deep into debt to his bankers.

He needed Ruth very much by the time she joined the circus.

10

The Show Must
Go On

I HAD BEEN RECUPERATING FOR MANY MONTHS FROM IN-
juries sustained in an automobile accident when Tom called
from San Angelo, Texas, and asked us to meet him there.

"He needs help," Ruth said. "I can tell by the tone of his
voice."

"Yes," I said. "We'd better get there quickly."

The circus was at that time in winter quarters at Texarkana, Texas. In another month the second-season tour would be
starting. We had heard from Tom frequently during the first
season, but he had carefully kept his difficulties hidden from
us. We were aware, however, that he was going through the
hardest period of his life.

In San Angelo he tried to be light about his hard luck.

"We had a little bad luck the first season," he said, smiling bravely, "but this year it's going to be different."

Actually he had had a great deal of misfortune that first season. Though his circus had played to capacity crowds once the first dreadful bouts with the weather were over, Tom was not able to make up the losses he had sustained during the first few weeks of the season.

There were factors other than the weather that contributed to his losses too. There was an epidemic among the animals, for instance, that destroyed a number of valuable horses and an elephant. One of the aerialists fell during the act, too, and was subjected to a spinal injury that incapacitated him permanently for circus work after that. Tom gave this man a large sum of money to cover his medical expenses and living costs until he could find some other means of making a living.

By the time the first season ended he had used all his capital. The big house in Beverly Hills had long been gone—and the yacht and string of Rolls Royces. He was literally a poor man despite the millions he had made as the highest paid star of the screen. He had negotiated a loan to carry the circus through winter quarters, and was beginning the second season under the duress of heavy debt.

Still, he didn't reveal to us the extent of his trouble during our talk in San Angelo. He was still looking forward to the future with courage.

"I think we've got a better show than last season's set up for this year," he said. He looked at Ruth and smiled wistfully. "But I can think of a way it can be made even better."

"Dad, if I can help—" Ruth began.

They both looked at me. Of course I hated to see Ruth go, especially since I wasn't fully recovered from my accident; but I knew how important this was to both Tom and Ruth.

I smiled. "What are we waiting for?" I said. "There are lots of plans to be made, aren't there?"

The tension seemed to ebb out of him right away. For the rest of the meal, while we made our plans, he seemed almost like the Tom Mix of the old happy days. But not quite. The old Tom Mix was really gone for good. Too many troubles had scarred him.

The following month was one of the happiest for Tom that he had spent in years. He and Ruth went to California where they perfected the routine they later performed together in the show. They worked long hours together every day and Ruth wrote me that his physical endurance was as awe-inspiring as ever, though he was in his late fifties by then.

Tom and Ruth returned to Texarkana just before the season was to start. With her at his side, Tom's spirits were substantially raised. His pep talk to his crew and performers was full of the old fire and hope.

And the first few weeks of the second season went well. The circus played to big crowds and Tom made enough money to meet expenses and begin to retire the heavy financial obligation he had undertaken. He continued to refuse financial help from me, for he knew that the foundation of his circus venture was still undeniably shaky. I did, however, buy Ruth her car and trailer in an effort to do something to help.

I was well enough by the time the show reached Austin, Texas, to go to see it. I had worried that perhaps Tom's financial troubles might affect his performances, but my fear was groundless. He was more brilliant than ever. His flash, fire and unexcelled physical aura dazzled the thousands of persons who came to see him wherever the circus played.

Perhaps he couldn't have done it that year if Ruth had not been with him. She was an integral part of his act, and his stature seemed to grow to even larger dimensions than usual when she was at his side. He performed all his marvelous tricks with even more agility and dash than before and he and Ruth, as a team, performed some new riding, shooting, and roping tricks that had the fans stamping and cheering.

I was thrilled for them. And at that moment I lost temporarily some of the ominous doubts I had felt about his circus venture.

At dinner that night I was cheerfully candid about it. "You have a brilliant show," I said, "and I'm sure you are going to come through on it this year."

Tom looked at Ruth and grinned. "Sure we are," he said. "All we need is a few good breaks this year."

It was a while before the breaks turned bad. There was no weather trouble at first. The fans turned out for the circus in droves. Naturally this good luck caused a regrowth of Tom's confidence in himself. It was evident that his immense popularity with his fans was still undiminished. Everywhere his circus played he had reunions with his old friends. Invariably he would honor these old friends by asking them to ride in the grand entry with Ruth and himself.

Colonel William Sterling, then Adjutant General of Texas, was a man so honored one day. Bill and Tom were old friends from the days when Tom had served in various capacities of law-enforcement work in the West. It was a very hot day. When Bill rode to town—his ranch was close to San Antonio, where the circus was playing that day—he dismounted at the show grounds and unsaddled the black-and-white quarter horse he was riding. The heat had caused the horse to sweat and some of the red coloring from the saddle blanket had run and clung to the horse.

"I don't think the heat did that at all," Tom said, laughing. "I think you're too big for that little horse, Bill. I think you pressed that coloring right into him."

Bill Sterling, being six feet four, did rather dwarf his horse.

Quarter horses are never very tall, and Bill's was no exception.

"You know, Bill," Tom laughed, "we can't have you riding that horse in the grand entry. I'm afraid your feet might drag on the ground!"

Tom insisted that Bill ride the beautiful black colt he had been training as a substitute for his own mount, Warrior. The colt was named Crow and he was a good seventeen hands tall. Colonel Sterling made an imposing sight on him in the grand entry. After the performance was over Tom made a gift of the horse to him.

"But I can't accept this horse," Colonel Sterling said. "Why, you've been training him for yourself."

"I've been training him for you," Tom said. "I've been figuring you'd be needing a new mount about now."

The Colonel had hundreds of horses on his ranch, and Tom certainly couldn't afford to part with a valuable animal like Crow at that time, but he wanted to make a gift to the Colonel.

Shortly after that afternoon, however, the bottom began to fall out of things again.

Business had been good. Tom had been steadily reducing the load of debt he was carrying and had begun to carry fresh hope inside him.

Then one day when the circus was playing at Auburn, California, a harbinger of disaster took hold in Tom's mind. That day he was very ill. He had been hospitalized countless times in his life for injuries and wounds sustained in his war adventures, law-enforcement work, and movie-making activities, but his inordinately robust health had always kept him safe from most of the ordinary illnesses of the body.

He wasn't safe from nerves. When Ruth stopped at his trailer a few minutes before the performance was to begin, she found him blanched and shaking.

He tried to smile. "Just a case of the jumps," he said. "Will you take the show for me today, Ruth?"

"We'll call the show off," Ruth said, her alarm growing rapidly. She had never seen her father this way before. No one else ever saw him that way.

"If you can just get the show started," he said, "maybe I can go on later."

"Dad, you need a doctor," Ruth said, anxiously. "We've got to call the show off. I—couldn't take your place."

Although he was shaking so hard he could scarcely stand up, Tom gripped her shoulders. "There has to be a Mix out there today, Ruth. We've never let them down yet, have we?"

Ruth was crying and feverish with worry when she left Tom to rush out to ask the advice of Johnny Agee.

"You look just like your father," he told her.

"You mean—that I should go out there and—?"

"Come on," he said. "Let's stick that long hair of yours under your hat."

Ruth in later years often told of making her entry on the great gelding, Warrior . . . how scared she was when the music started and she rode into the big tent. But she got away with it! Apparently the audience thought they were seeing the real Tom Mix. Fortunately Tom recovered sufficiently to do his many stunts.

Another disaster was waiting at a small city in Montana. The circus moved into town and made the usual preparations to set up for the performances. The circus lot was already overrun with youngsters clamoring for Tom's autograph when a couple of town officials arrived to see him.

It was a tough town. The officials looked as though they belonged there. They elbowed their way through the group of youngsters that were crowding around Tom.

"Gotta see you," one of them told Tom curtly.

Tom tried to be gracious. "Sure," he said, "but there's some work to be finished first."

By the time Tom finished the autographs and did a few lasso tricks for his eager young fans, the two officials were fidgeting impatiently.

"All right," Tom said. "What can I do for you men?"

"Just this," said one of them. "We want two hundred complimentary tickets for town officials and their families and friends. It's the custom around here when a show comes to town." The man's eyes narrowed. "In fact, it's a kind of law."

Tom smiled. "Sounds like a funny law to me. Seems as if the town officials, who have jobs, at least could afford to buy tickets for their families and friends." He kept right on smiling. "You see, we keep our admission charge as low as possible so as many persons as possible can see the show. We have a law too. Our complimentary tickets go to underprivileged children and to charitable organizations."

"I'd advise you to change your rule in this case," the official said with an ugly grimace.

"Sorry," said Tom, still smiling.

"Can't guarantee your show'll be very safe," the man said.

Tom shrugged and turned away from the man. He could not be coerced or intimidated. He could not violate his principles of right and wrong in any circumstances.

That night, an hour before the performance was due to begin, the "wrecking crew" arrived, led by the two men who had approached Tom that morning. Their angry followers were other "officials" and a group of hoboes they had rallied behind them. It was a mob at work, a mob frenzied by all the taut emotionalism attendant on the Depression.

Tom and his circus crew fought valiantly in one of the biggest mass fist fights of all time. They were soon overwhelmed by sheer force of number. The mob ripped the big tent and tore it down. Trailers and cars were overturned and wrecked. In the violence, several valuable horses were killed, and a number of Tom's men were severely injured.

It was all over very quickly. What a few minutes before had been a color-flamed invitation to excitement and entertainment was now the ruin of a dream. It was as if a gigantic scythe had passed over the circus grounds, destroying everything with one titantic sweep.

Tom and Ruth were up all night helping the injured. There were a number of bruised and cut bodies, but fortunately none of the circus crew were so seriously hurt that the circus couldn't move out of town the next morning.

A great amount of equipment had been wrecked beyond salvage. What was still usable or repairable was loaded into the vehicles that hadn't been destroyed, and the circus left town at dawn.

Just before they pulled out, Tom gathered the discouraged circus personnel together.

"We'll build the show again," he said firmly. "We've got to do it—and we *will* do it."

There was one more bitter piece of luck to endure before they reached the next town on their schedule. A truck pulling a trailerful of horses went out of control on a mountain road and plunged into a ravine, killing several horses and injuring the driver badly. The total loss from the whole misfortune was fantastic. Most people would have given up. But not Tom.

Up until that night he had succeeded in reducing substantially the heavy debt he had been carrying. With the mob disaster, he was forced to assume new and even heavier obligations to get started again.

Everyone worked hard to repair the damages and Tom, on

the basis of his good name and reputation for honesty, got quick financing for some new equipment. The circus was ready to resume its schedule within three weeks, but the losses alone from the failure to meet playing dates during the idle period were enormous.

For a long time after that, things went along on a slow up-hill grade again. The killing blow was yet to come.

It was a beautiful day. Spring had come unseasonably early to Neenah, Wisconsin. There was a bright sun and a rash of new spring hats. The town was abuzz with excitement, not only over this brash burgeoning of spring, but also because the Tom Mix Circus had just hit town.

The day wore by in warm gentleness. The air seemed to be thick and sultry. No one was aware that the unusual blandness was a black harbinger of what was to befall that evening.

The rain started just after the performance began. It started with gentle brushing at first, and the audience that packed the tent was hardly aware that it was raining at all.

Tom and Ruth had made their triumphant exit from their first act and had gone to their trailers to change for the next act. Ruth was hurrying to Tom's trailer with a scarf she had washed for him when the wind struck. It came scurrying through the grounds like a preliminary whip crack at first and then, suddenly, it crashed upon them—a violent crash between warm air and cold, a tornado!

Ruth was practically blown into Tom's trailer.

"The animals!" Tom shouted over the scream of wind. "Cut them loose and then come to the big tent."

Ruth beat against the wind, thinking she was going to be ripped apart, but she finally reached the tent where the animals—the llamas, zebras, shetland ponies, and horses—were stabled and tied. She and some of the circus crew worked frantically to get the animals freed before their tent sagged and crashed down under the heavy force of wind and the lash of rain.

By the time Ruth had reached the big performance tent, it had partly collapsed. The interior equipment was fortunately too large to allow a complete collapse, but the crowd was swept with hysteria and was milling around helplessly despite Tom's desperate attempts, from his station in the center ring, to empty the tent with a semblance of order. He stood there trying to allay fear, but the feeling of panic was infectious and the exits were soon jammed by a frantic mob that could move neither forward nor backward. The melee was made all the more uncontrollable by the horses and elephants, which were in the center ring when the storm struck and which, too, were milling around in fright among the yelling crowd.

The fire department arrived and cut long rents in the tent in an effort to get the people out.

The tornado abated as swiftly as it had begun. Suddenly there was no wind, only a light, cold drizzle. Gradually, with Tom's persuasive voice over the loud-speaker helping matters considerably, the tent was emptied in a reasonably ordered manner. Miraculously there were few spectators seriously injured.

Instead of brooding over the financial ruin the tornado disaster had brought him, Tom spent most of the rest of the night helping a woman look for her child, who had been lost in the stampede of the crowd. Near dawn the child was found wandering in a field.

He came back to the circus grounds to face a dejected circus crew. In his moment of great loss he said something typical of him: "We have everything to be thankful for. No lives were lost and no one was badly injured. Now let's get to work."

They all got to work, Tom included, sewing up the tent rents and repairing the equipment damaged by the storm.

But the Tom Mix Circus was beyond mending.

Tom had been approached to make another tour of Europe. His great popularity there had begun in 1915, when Aubert of France took over the distribution of a long list of his Selig films for exhibition on the Continent. Tom's pictures were huge money-makers in foreign countries for years after that and were still doing splendidly. He was the personification of the Great Good Western Man to millions of European youngsters as well as to millions of American junior cowboys.

That first European personal appearance tour of his was a great success. The enthusiastic followers that gathered at Le Havre to meet his ship could not restrain their joy when Tom, dressed in one of his brilliant cowboy outfits, rode down the unloading ramp of the steamer on his horse and pressed right into the crowds. He literally entered Europe on horseback, a very fitting act for the most famous cowboy in the world. He was delayed there by the besieging crowd for almost four hours before they released him to catch a train to Paris where he was to do his first European show.

In Paris he rode in the streets for hours while the fans lined the boulevards and cheered him; and of course his performance there had been sold out for weeks in advance. It was like that in every European capital he played.

There was every indication that the financial success of the tour proposed in 1938 would be every bit as overwhelming as that of the first one. It looked like a sure way for Tom to step out of his financial bog.

"I think it's the best thing to do," Tom told Ruth. "We can get our debts cleared off—and then we can start fresh again."

For the circus was floundering in debt by then. Ever since it had twice been almost totally destroyed—first by the mob in Montana and then by the tornado in Wisconsin—Tom's efforts to get on his feet had been stymied in every direction.

"Of course," he told Ruth, "I won't make the tour unless you come along."

Ruth was thrilled with the idea and she and Tom were busy making plans from then on. While the agents were at work making the final arrangements for the tour, Tom was planning to put the circus in cold storage until his profits from the foreign tour enabled him to retire all existing obligations against the show and then resume on a debt-free basis. Ruth thought everything was settled.

Then one night after they concluded a performance in an old town in New England, Tom showed up at Ruth's trailer looking pale and distraught. At that moment he seemed old for the first time in his life.

"Will you go for a drive with me, Ruth?" he said in a voice that was strangely quavering. "I know it's late and I know you're tired, but I think I've got to talk to you tonight."

"Why, of course," she said.

They drove about a mile out of town to a Revolutionary War cemetery that rolled down from a verdant knoll to an ancient river. It was a beautiful, peaceful night with a full moon making a silvered tracery of the riverbank trees in the water. But Ruth was nervously watching Tom's ashen face and his restless dark eyes.

They sat down on the riverbank and Tom turned to face Ruth. "I've sure made a botch of things for us, haven't I?" he said.

"Don't talk like that," Ruth said quietly. "We have everything to look forward to now. The European tour will solve all our problems."

"I'm not so sure," Tom said in a strained voice. "I'm not so sure."

Ruth leaned toward him and put her hand on his arm. "Dad, what's wrong?" If *you've* given up hope, why there's just no hope for any of us."

He tried to smile. "I don't think I'm a very good one for giving hope to anyone," he said. "It seems a little fantastic that I've reached this stage of life only to end up a failure."

Ruth twisted uncomfortably. "A failure? After what you've given the world? How can you even think that?"

"A personal failure," he said. "I've failed my family. And in doing that I've failed myself."

Ruth tried to protest. "Circumstances were against the family life you really wanted," she said.

"They didn't have to be," he returned. "When you were a baby, Ruth, I kept thinking that one day we'd be living in our own little world, as a family should. But I kept putting off that day until it was suddenly too late."

Ruth remonstrated. "Why think about something that can't be done over, Dad?" She took his hand in hers affectionately. "There's the future. You've always thought about the future—remember?"

This ebbing out of the inner feelings that had been accumulating in Tom for years was as difficult for Ruth as it was for him. All his life he had secluded his troubles deep within himself, refusing to share them even with those closest to him. But now he had reached a point where his need for understanding overpowered his desire not to hurt others. He had tallied his life and concluded that he had lost somewhere his own touch with happiness and with it the ability to make others happy.

"Sure, there's always the future," he agreed, trying to smile and not quite managing. "But when you reach a certain point . . . well, the future is compounded of the past too." He straightened a little. "Where I've failed, I'm sure you can carry on, Ruth."

She was silent, but she did not understand the signficance of that remark right then.

Tom stood up and looked down at her. "Ruth, I guess there's

one thing about life that keeps us tough and urges us on, and that's doing things we don't want to do. I hope you'll remember that in the morning." He turned his face away. "I think I need to be alone for a few minutes. Think I'll take a little walk."

"All right," said Ruth quietly. "I'll be waiting here."

She watched him as he walked up the slope, through the cemetery, and into a wood of ancient trees. She waited . . . and waited. It seemed as though hours passed before she heard a car start with a muffled blast of its exhaust.

Ruth ran up the slope and found that her father, in his distraught condition, had simply forgotten she was there. Or had he? Anyway, he had driven away alone.

On her mile walk back to town, she cried all the way. She felt that she had been completely inadequate in her attempt to help her father in the greatest moment of stress in his life. She had a feeling that their talk had been abortive. There was so much more that needed to be said. Yet when she reached the circus grounds and went to Tom's trailer, she found him deep in a sleep of emotional exhaustion. She did not awaken him. Slipping quietly away, she went to her own trailer. In the morning, she felt, they would continue their talk, and this time she would find some way to help her father get his perspective in focus again.

But in the morning Tom was gone.

Through blurring eyes, she read the note he had left for her:

I'm off for Europe, Ruth. I tried to tell you last night that I'd have to do this alone—but I just couldn't do it. You see, the creditors insist that a Mix stay with the circus while I'm in Europe. I know you're going to bring it through for us. After our talk last night . . . now I'm sure there *is* a future.

Ruth rallied under the faith her father had in her. Her responsibilities became immediately huge, but she faced them with resolute courage. She wanted her father to be as proud of her as she was of him. She knew how difficult it had been for him to leave her during the most crucial moment of his life.

Some day he would come back, she thought, with his future resolved and his strength reborn in him.

Tom eventually did come back from Europe. But that night on the bank of a quiet New England river was the last time Ruth ever saw her father alive.

11 ᴄ⌣

Ring Down
the Curtain

THE TOM MIX CIRCUS STARRING RUTH MIX KEPT STRUG-
gling on the road for the rest of the season.

Ruth had nothing to fear about audience reception to her
act. Tom Mix's daughter had become a Big Name in her own
right. There was only one Tom Mix in the world, of course,
but Ruth came as close to stepping into her father's boots as
anyone could. After years of practicing and of modeling herself after her father, she was able to perform his daring tricks
and remarkable skills with a finesse and an obliviousness of
danger very closely approaching his.

She tried her very hardest to keep the faltering enterprise

going. Perhaps, given another season and a fresh start, she could have pulled the circus out of its financial chaos. But the creditors were very wary. The country was in the grip of another economic dip, and keeping the circus going would have required a fresh investment of capital that the creditors were not willing to assume.

The death of the Tom Mix Circus was a sad and terrible thing. I went to Pecos, Texas, to see the final performance, and was acutely aware that Ruth, despite the smile she carried all during her act, was sick with grief. My own eyes were heavy with tears. When the crowd poured out of the tent that night it was as though the final curtain had been run down on Tom's life. Ruth and I did something we had never done before. We wept in each other's arms.

They began to dismantle the equipment after the performance. It was to be sold as soon as possible so that a portion of the debts could be satisfied.

We left the grounds immediately after the show and tried to eat a late supper. But our food was untouched.

"I'm glad Daddy wasn't here to see it die," Ruth said.

"Your father has triumphed over a lot of disappointments in his life," I said with confidence. "I don't think this one will be any exception."

I was right. We wrote the full particulars of the closing of the circus to Tom. His answer came from Europe quickly. He was grieved, of course, that the circus had folded before he returned from Europe and might be in a position to buoy its foundations with the money he was making through his personal appearance tour; but he was confident that he and Ruth could get a fresh start with the show when he returned. He told of the tremendous success he was having in Europe and hoped that soon again he would be able to rehire his old friends who had been let out of jobs by the closing of the circus.

We knew then that he was thinking of the future, that the old confidence and zest for life still burned within him.

The death of the circus brought a new life for Ruth. She found time to think over a proposal of marriage from an old suitor, Sheriff Howard Cragg, of Raymondville, Texas. They were married, and she and her husband settled on his ranch in the Rio Grande Valley. She was there when Tom came home from Europe.

Upon arriving in New York, Tom tried to telephone Ruth immediately; but Ruth's husband was in the process of building the ranch house and no telephone had been installed as yet. Tom telegraphed Ruth to call him.

When she reached him she found that his voice was full of the verve and ebullience of the old days.

"I've just had the most fun I've had in a long time," he said. "I arranged with my bankers here to pay off all my old debts. The slate's wiped clean, Ruth!"

We had heard of the fabulous success of Tom's tour in foreign countries; however, we had known, too, from the tone of his letters that he had been lonely in Europe despite his immense popularity over there. It was ironic that a man so famous could be so alone. No doubt he tolerated the loneliness simply to make sufficient money to retire his debts.

"I'll see you in a few days," Tom said. "I'm driving to the coast to talk over a picture deal. I'm stopping in Chicago to discuss a personal appearance tour in South America too. Things look pretty bright, Ruth!"

Ruth almost choked with her happiness. "You see, Dad," she said, "you didn't lose your touch with the future after all. I knew you wouldn't."

"I'm all right now," Tom assured her. "But the future's going to look even brighter when I see you. It'll only be a few days, chicken." It was like old times for Tom to use his pet name for Ruth—"chicken."

It was over a week later that he telephoned Ruth from Tucson, Arizona. The call came through to a filling station a few miles from Ruth's ranch and the proprietor took a message from Tom asking Ruth to call him at his hotel in Tucson.

"Great news!" he said exuberantly when Ruth returned his call. "The deal is practically set up for South America! A year's contract starting in February. That'll give me time to finish the picture in Hollywood if it looks like a good thing."

"Wonderful!" Ruth said.

"That isn't all," he went on. "I couldn't be any happier if you and your husband would plan to come along on the South American tour. This time there won't be any creditors breathing down our necks and breaking up the Mix team."

"Oh, I don't know," said Ruth hesitantly. "I guess I've given up show business, Dad."

But Tom's enthusiasm over the idea couldn't be subdued.

"I have to leave for Hollywood tomorrow, because there's a rush on this film contract. Can you and Howard come out and join me? We can talk it over then."

Ruth made a quick decision. "Yes," she said. "We'll leave for California tomorrow."

"Seeing you again will make me the happiest man in the world," Tom told her. There was a long pause and Ruth thought there was something wrong with the connection. But her father's voice came again, this time deep and vibrant. "You know, Ruthie, it took a lot of things and a long time to learn. I've been a great success in one way and an utter failure in others . . . but now . . . now that I know the ones who really love me now and always have . . ."

Tom's voice broke off. "Oh, Daddy!" said Ruth. She was so affected it was all she could say.

Tom's penchant for fast, sporty cars had not dimmed over the years. After the phone call to Ruth he jumped into his white Cord convertible to drive to California. It was the morning of October 12, 1940.

No doubt he was driving fast. He always drove at top speed. The narrow ribbon of road that stretched over a seemingly limitless expanse of land was practically unbroken by traffic or road impediments.

Probably his mind was on the future as he drove along and he failed to give attention to the sudden rise in the road that amounted almost to a hill. He must have slowed down a bit, for the hill obstructed forward vision, but he did not slow down enough.

When he came to the top of the hill a partly constructed bridge that was being built across a gully loomed up before him.

There had been no warning sign posted, and he was totally unprepared for the obstruction. He turned instantly to start down the steep detour road that crossed the gully. But the sharp turn and steep angle of declivity loosened the heavy suitcase on the rack behind his head. It came crashing against his neck. He died instantly.

The car came to rest at the bottom of the gully, and a passing motorist discovered Tom's body a few minutes after the accident. He was lying across the seat of the car and the repose on his face indicated that death had come painlessly.

There was a note in the pocket of his jacket from the hotel of Tucson to the effect that Ruth would call him at eight-thirty from Raymondville. There was no other address to be found. At the time of his death he was a man without a home.

Tom, who had escaped death by a wisp of margin hundreds of times in his life, met his death from an inanimate object that in ordinary circumstances would have been harmless— a suitcase. It is true that Ruth and I, over the years, had always expected Tom's death at any moment. We had expected his death to be abrupt and sudden when it came, but we were shocked and overwhelmed when it finally occurred. The most pathetic aspect of it was that his passing had come at a time when he was, after all those bleak years, just beginning to recapture the glory of his former life.

He was sixty years old when he died. He had lived a full life, but had he lived on, there was so much more he could have done. When he died he was as physically fit as he had been at thirty. But, most important, his hope was full of youth too.